Behavioural Economics
and Policy Design

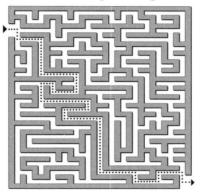

Examples from Singapore

Behavioural Economics
and Policy Design

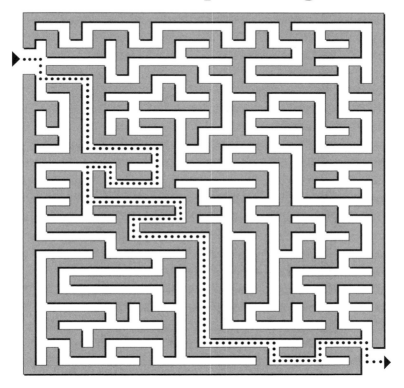

Examples from Singapore

Edited by

Donald Low

Civil
Service
College
Singapore

World Scientific

Published by

World Scientific Publishing Co. Pte. Ltd.

5 Toh Tuck Link, Singapore 596224

USA office: 27 Warren Street, Suite 401-402, Hackensack, NJ 07601

UK office: 57 Shelton Street, Covent Garden, London WC2H 9HE

Library of Congress Cataloging-in-Publication Data
Behavioural economics and policy design : examples from Singapore / edited by Donald Low.
   p. cm.
  Includes bibliographical references and index.
  ISBN-13: 978-9814366007
  ISBN-10: 9814366005
  1. Singapore--Economic policy--Case studies. 2. Economics--Psychological aspects--
Case studies. I. Low, Donald, 1973–   II. Civil Service College, Singapore.
  HC445.8.B45 2011
  330.01'9--dc23

               2011038079

British Library Cataloguing-in-Publication Data
A catalogue record for this book is available from the British Library.

ISBN-13 978-981-4366-00-7
ISBN-10 981-4366-00-5

In-house Editor: Agnes Ng

Typeset by Stallion Press
Email: enquiries@stallionpress.com

Printed in Singapore by World Scientific Printers.

"Academics place much more importance on rigorous logic. There is also admiration in the profession for subtle reasoning. And mastery of the craft shows itself in the elegance of the intellectual super-structure. ... The practitioner, on the other hand, uses economic theory only to the extent that he finds it useful in comprehending the problem at hand, so that practical courses of action will emerge which can be evaluated not merely in narrow economic cost-benefit terms, but by taking into account a wider range of considerations. ... A practitioner is not judged by the rigour of his logic or by the elegance of his presentation. He is judged by results."

Goh Keng Swee

"The world is better served by syncretic economists and policymakers who can hold multiple ideas in their heads than by 'one-handed' economists who promote one big idea regardless of context."

Dani Rodrik

FOREWORD

Recent events suggest that we are living in an era of increased turbulence. Take for example the wide-ranging impacts of the 1998 Asian financial crisis, the terrorist attacks of September 11, the Severe Acute Respiratory Syndrome (SARS) epidemic in 2003 and the 2008/2009 credit crisis. The common thread running across each of these crises is that they were all not foreseen sufficiently early. Yet it was not the lack of information or the absence of early warning signs that caused governments and businesses to mostly ignore the risks of an impending crisis. Indeed, the crises were predictable, or at least, they should have been better anticipated. So why weren't they?

The research that has emerged from complex systems suggests that much of our failure to have anticipated these and other low-probability, high-impact events has to do with the way we perceive and analyse the world. The standard approaches we use to assess risks are usually based on linear causal relationships, derived from past experience. These approaches assume — implicitly — that the world is governed by definite and repeatable cause-and-effect relationships. They fail to take into account the *external* reality of complexity and inherent unpredictability, which suggests that many of the problems we face cannot be reduced to simple and precise cause-and-effect relationships. The weather, the economy and the natural world are examples of complex systems. Such systems exhibit regularity without being entirely predictable. They are capable of producing entirely new and unexpected forms of behaviour. In complex systems, the relationship between cause and effect is not as consistent as in the regular, simple systems we are familiar in dealing with.

At the same time, the research from cognitive psychology and behavioural economics suggests that the standard economic approaches we are familiar with also fail to account for people's *internal* limitations in handling probabilities and in managing risk and uncertainty. Conventional economics, for instance, starts with the assumption that people are rational agents capable of maximising their interests and of calculating the pros and cons of their decisions in a cool and dispassionate way. The reality — as behavioural economists and cognitive psychologists have discovered — is far more complicated.

In recent years, behavioural economists have begun to apply Plato's idea that human beings have two distinct decision-making systems. When confronted with situations that require us to make decisions in a short span of time, we think in ways that are quite different than if we are given more time to make up our minds. We use the Automatic System to deal with matters that require quick decisions. The Automatic System, as the name suggests, is intuitive, unconscious (in that we make decisions even without knowing that we are making them), uncontrolled, effortless, habitual, and based on practice skills. This is the system of thinking we use in our day-to-day activities and when we have only a short time to make decisions.

When we have sufficient time for reflection and to process the information presented to us, we rely more on the Reflective System. This mode of thinking is controlled, slow, deliberate, conscious and effortful. Most of what we are taught in schools, our reasoning and analytical skills, as well as the scientific method, is based on the Reflective System. The economics that we were taught in schools and universities is also based on the assumption of rational consumers and firms making decisions using the Reflective System.

How different are these two systems of thought? Consider and answer this question as quickly as you can:

> The combined cost of a ball and a bat is $1.10 and the bat costs $1 more than the ball. What is the price of the ball?

If you answered ten cents, do not be surprised. The large majority of people who have taken this test also answered "ten cents". That is the result of the Automatic System. It takes a deliberate effort to override this automatic response. If you had more time to answer the question, your Reflective System would have arrived at the correct answer of five cents.

The problem is not that we have two systems of thinking and decision making. The problem arises when we rely on one system in situations when we should be using the other system. For example, if you are faced with a decision that requires you to assess risks and probabilities — such as which health insurance plan you should purchase — you ought to rely on your Reflective System. Relying on your instincts to deal with a problem which you are not familiar and have little prior experience with will probably result in poor decisions.

There are other occasions when our decisions deviate from what rational choice models in standard economics prescribe. A well known finding from behavioural economics is that people value losses more heavily than gains of the same size. Thus they value more highly a programme that restores a loss than one which provides them a gain of the same size. Similarly, they cite a much higher price to give up something they already possess as compared to the price which they are prepared to pay for exactly the same thing that they do not have.

Why do these deviations from standard economics matter for policymakers? There are at least two levels in which policymakers should take the insights of behavioural economics seriously. At one level, policymakers should appreciate the various ways in which people make decisions that depart — predictably and regularly — from the strict tenets of rationality. Behavioural economists have documented a number of cognitive biases and mental traits that can skew people's judgements of probability and uncertainty. For instance, procrastination, laziness or unfamiliarity with alternatives often lead to people having a strong bias in favour of the status quo in their choice of investment or savings plan. Knowing this, social security policymakers should think carefully about the defaults that are assigned to citizens, since it is quite likely that the average citizen will stick with whatever choice is set for him.

Behavioural economists have also found that people have a general inclination to judge things relative to some arbitrary reference point — this is known as the anchoring bias. For example, if a person is exposed to a high number just before he makes a purchase, he tends to be willing to pay a higher price than if he were subject to a low number, even if the number has nothing to do with the object being considered for purchase. How problems or options are framed to citizens can also have an important bearing on people's responses. People are more likely to accept a programme that has a 90% success rate than one which has a 10% failure rate, even though both statements carry identical information. Policymakers should be conscious of how citizens' responses can be altered — sometimes quite significantly — by different ways in which information or choices are presented to them.

At this level of analysis, behavioural economics can help policymakers *structure* choices and information for their citizens in ways that take into account their cognitive biases and complications. By offering governments a more realistic understanding of how people decide under conditions of risk, uncertainty and complexity, behavioural economics provides governments with the means to design policies that are sensitive to people's psychology.

At another level, behavioural economics can also help governments to be more self-aware and to assess the risks they face more rigorously. The same cognitive biases that behavioural economists say ordinary citizens are affected by may also apply to policymakers and decision-makers in government. For instance, just as the average citizen may get anchored on a certain argument or number, so too may policymakers cling to their prevailing assumptions by mistakenly interpreting any evidence as supportive even if it is actually contradictory. This tendency to rationalise things in terms we are familiar or comfortable with can lead to governments (or other organisations) being blindsided by risks or problems that they have not contemplated before. The failure of most mainstream economists to anticipate the financial crisis of 2008 is a case in point. Most of them did not question the prevailing wisdom of the times — that we were living in an era of the Great Moderation (low inflation, sustained growth), that central banks had figured out how to stabilise the economy, and that financial innovation had diversified and reduced risks — and were therefore caught out by the crisis.

Related to this is the tendency of the human mind to see what it wants to see and to ignore evidence that contradicts its beliefs. This confirmation bias, combined with over-confidence (another mental trait that behavioural economists have identified), can lead to hubris and the inability to imagine that something very bad could happen — a phenomenon known as "disaster myopia". Disaster myopia afflicts organisations as much as it does individuals. The lesson for governments in all this is to remember the motto of Delphi — "Know Thyself" — and to understand the role that emotions and cognitive biases play in our decision-making processes.

This book is a valuable contribution to the discussion on how behavioural economics can help governments do better — both in terms of designing policies that accommodate people's cognitive biases as well as being conscious of their own. Good ideas in public policy are not developed in the laboratory. They must take into account how the ideas are translated into implementable, enforceable and accepted policies. Singapore's experience is useful in this regard. As many of the chapters here attest, there was a conscious effort on the part of Singapore's policymakers to incorporate people's likely responses and reactions into the design of policies. Even when policies are grounded in sound economic logic, there is no guarantee that they will be widely accepted. Often, they have to be tweaked, adjusted or significantly reframed to ensure public acceptance. The combination of standard economic principles and insights from behavioural economics is an important contributing factor to sound public policies in Singapore.

Having encouraged the Civil Service College, Singapore to expand its repertoire of programmes to include behavioural economics and its applications in public policy, I am heartened to see the publication of this book. I am also thankful that my colleagues in the civil service have made a great effort to bring these examples of complex policy formulation into the public domain. Their effort is worthwhile as it will bring about a greater appreciation of the value of behavioural economics in public administration. The book will be an important source of cases for the teaching of behavioural economics at the college. It will also provide ideas on how behavioural economics and, more generally, insights from the cognitive sciences can be of value to governments. Finally, I hope the book will encourage readers to reflect on how public policies can be improved and refined as we understand human behaviour better.

Lam Chuan Leong

Ambassador-at-large

Ministry of Foreign Affairs

and

Senior Fellow

Civil Service College, Singapore

Acknowledgements

This book would not have been possible without a great deal of help from many people. I would like to record my thanks to all the contributors from the Singapore government who took time to write in their personal capacity. Not only did they take up the challenge of writing about a relatively unexplored subject, they also had to put up with my incessant questions and numerous revisions to their drafts. Wendy Wong of the Civil Service College, Singapore and Cheryl Chung of the Ministry of Trade and Industry painstakingly conceptualised and developed the illustrations in this book. I am grateful for their patience and hard work.

I owe a huge debt of gratitude to two individuals. The first is Professor Jack Knetsch, Emeritus Professor of Economics at Simon Fraser University. Professor Knetsch is one of the pioneers in behavioural economics. As a Senior Visiting Fellow of the Civil Service College, he helped to establish the college's training and research programmes in behavioural economics and public policy. He provided wise counsel throughout the entire journey of this book — from its conceptualisation, to the identification of chapters, to providing specific ideas on how each of them could be made more credible and persuasive. The second individual is Dawn Yip who tirelessly read through early drafts of the chapters and provided valuable editorial and content inputs.

I would also like to thank my former colleagues at the Civil Service College. The former and current deans of the college — Chan Heng Kee and Lionel Yeo respectively — encouraged me to advance economics literacy in the Singapore public service. My colleagues — especially Tan Li San, Chng Kai Fong, Low Chee Seng, Wu Wei Neng, Sharon Tham, Christian Chao, Andrew Kwok,

Gabriel Wong, Pamela Qiu and Song Hsi Ching — provided ideas and a listening ear. The fellows at the college's Centre for Public Economics — David Skilling, Manu Bhaskaran, Yeoh Lam Keong and Lawrence Wong — were also extremely generous with their time and advice.

Outside of the college, I had the privilege of working with some of the best minds in the Singapore public service: Lim Siong Guan, Peter Ho, Ravi Menon, Lam Chuan Leong, Yong Ying-I, Chan Lai Fung, Philip Ong, Lai Wei Lin, Tai Wei Shyong, Chia Der Jiun, Francis Chong, Edward Robinson, Lee Kok Fatt, Dominic Soon, Devadas Krishnadas, Koh Tsin Yen, Keith Tan, Thia Jang Ping, Yip Chun Seng, Jeffrey Siow, Neo Bee Leng, Amanda Chua, Valerie Yuen, Godwin Tang, Bernard Toh, Sheila Pakir, Jeanette Kwek and Liu Feng-yuan. They gave me plenty of food for thought and abundant opportunities for intellectual sparring — not just for this book, but also in many other aspects of public policy. Sam Lam and Alan Sim at Linkage Asia encouraged me to bring the ideas of behavioural economics to audiences outside of the government, while Professors Neo Boon Siong and Henri Ghesquiere — the authors of two excellent books on the Singapore government — gave valuable suggestions on what policymakers elsewhere and students of government might find useful about Singapore's experience.

From my former perch at the Centre for Public Economics, I also had the privilege of engaging with some of the world's most creative economists and policy intellectuals: Paul Romer, Robert Frank, Ed Lazear, Arvind Subramaniam, Andrew Sheng, Bryan Caplan, Kenneth Lieberthal, Huang Yasheng, Linda Lim, Dani Rodrik, John Cassidy and Anatole Kaletsky. They provided thought-provoking insights and challenged my own assumptions and biases.

Donald Low
30 April 2011

CONTENTS

About the Authors

Jack KNETSCH is Emeritus Professor of Economics at Simon Fraser University and has held recent appointments as a Senior Visiting Fellow at the Civil Service College, Singapore and the Nanyang Visiting Professor at the Nanyang Technological University. His research on behavioural economics and applications to policy issues, extending over three decades, has appeared in most leading international journals. His name continues to appear regularly on lists of the most cited economists.

KOH Tsin Yen heads the Social Strategy Unit at the Ministry of Finance (MOF), Singapore, which studies medium-term social trends and issues and identifies gaps in the provision of social services. She has worked on a range of social policy and research issues in MOF and the Civil Service College, including subsidies for public housing and public education, assistance schemes for lower-income households, and changes to the social security system in Singapore.

LEONG Wai Yan served as a senior economist with the Policy and Planning Group of the Land Transport Authority (LTA), Singapore from 2008 to 2010. While at the LTA, he researched a wide array of land transport issues, such as cost-benefit analyses of rail projects and the impact of congestion pricing on motorists' behaviour. He has contributed substantively in the area of stated preference surveys and discrete choice modelling, including the updating of key economic parameters such as willingness-to-pay measures. In the course of his work, he developed a keen interest in behavioural economics and its applications to land transport policies. Mr. Leong holds a first class honours degree in Economics from Princeton University and a Masters in Economics from Stanford University. He is currently pursuing his PhD at the University of Sydney.

LEW Yii Der is the Group Director of the Policy and Planning Group of the Land Transport Authority (LTA), Singapore. His current portfolio includes studying reforms to the public transport industry structure and expanding the research and training capacity of the LTA Academy. Yii Der has been with the LTA since its formation in 1995 and has held various management positions. He holds a first class honours degree in Civil Engineering from the National University of Singapore and a Masters in Public Management from the Lee Kuan Yew School of Public Policy.

Donald LOW helped to establish the Centre for Public Economics at the Civil Service College, Singapore in 2009 and served as its first head for two years. The centre's role is to advance economics literacy in the Singapore public service through its training, outreach and research programmes. Prior to joining the college, he served in various capacities in the Singapore government. He was formerly the Director of Fiscal Policy at the Ministry of Finance, as well as the Director of the Strategic Policy Office in the Public Service Division. He is currently a vice president at the Economics Society of Singapore. Donald holds a first class honours degree in Politics, Philosophy and Economics from Oxford and a Masters in International Public Policy from Johns Hopkins University's School of Advanced International Studies.

Lavinia LOW is Assistant Director in Finance Policy at the Ministry of Health, Singapore. Her work includes policy development for MediShield (a basic catastrophic illness insurance scheme), the regulation of Medisave-approved insurance schemes, as well as the administration and regulation of ElderShield (a basic severe disability insurance scheme) and its supplementary plans.

Vivienne LOW is an analyst from the Policy and Planning Department of the Energy Market Authority, Singapore. She graduated from the National University of Singapore with a degree in Economics. She is currently responsible for the analysis of global trends and developments in energy, as well as the formulation of policies and strategies to facilitate the development of smart grids in Singapore.

Philip ONG is Director, Environmental Policy at the Ministry of Environment and Water Resources, Singapore. He is responsible for the review and formulation of policies on resource efficiency and environmental protection to support public health, sustainable development and a better quality of life. He joined the Ministry in 2008, initially covering climate change and energy efficiency issues, before overseeing environmental policies in 2009.

Pamela QIU joined the Centre for Public Economics at the Civil Service College, Singapore as a researcher from 2009 to 2011. Her areas of research included the economics of privatisation, regulation and competition policy, as well as fiscal management and social spending. From 2007 to 2009, she was an associate (Social Strategy) at the Ministry of Finance (MOF) where she worked on developing long-term strategies to improve the social services sector. The issues she worked closely on while at MOF included human capital development, reducing under-employment and facilitating social entrepreneurship.

Charmaine TAN is currently a research associate at the Centre for Public Economics at the Civil Service College, Singapore. Her research interests include the economics of industrial organization, regulation, competition policy and behavioural economics. She graduated with a BSc (Hons) in Economics from the National University of Singapore and a Masters in Economics of Markets and Organisations (Research) from the Toulouse School of Economics.

TAN Li San is Director of the Centre for Governance and Leadership at the Civil Service College, Singapore. She is concurrently Director of the Strategic Policy Office, including the Centre for Strategic Futures which helps to develop futures-planning capabilities across the Singapore public service. Li San has held various government positions during her career, including a stint at the Ministry of Finance from 2005 to 2009 where, as Director of the Social Programmes Directorate, she was responsible for the allocation of fiscal resources within the social sector.

Eugene TOH is Deputy Director of the Policy and Planning Department in the Energy Market Authority, Singapore. He graduated with a Masters in Electrical and Computer Engineering (ECE) from Carnegie Mellon University, USA and has a double first class Bachelor's degree in Economics and Philosophy, and ECE from the same institution. Prior to joining the Energy Planning and Development Division, he specialised in the regulation of competitive energy markets as Deputy Director of the EMA's Market Development and Surveillance Department. He is also concurrently the Deputy Project Director of the Intelligent Energy System pilot project, an initiative to develop the smart grid infrastructure and its applications for potential deployment in Singapore.

YEE Yiling is a health policy analyst in Finance Policy at the Ministry of Health, Singapore. Her work includes the administration and regulation of ElderShield and its supplementary plans, as well as the study of micro and macroeconomic perspectives of healthcare financing issues.

INTRODUCTION

COGNITION, CHOICE AND POLICY DESIGN

Donald LOW

"Economists are starting to abandon their assumption that humans behave rationally, and instead are finally coming to grips with the crazy, mixed up creatures we really are."

The Economist (16 December 1999)

"Behavioural economics has started to paint a more realistic picture. ... At first the findings seem to be anomalies and oddities, but on closer inspection they yield new principles and regularities."

Pete Lunn, *Prospect Magazine* (September 2008)

"... the primary target of our argument is not economists, but governmental leaders, policymakers and the public at large, to whom the message is that an over-reliance on (often mythical) economic assumptions and the over-generalisation and over-extension of economic principles in a variety of policy domains can have detrimental, if not disastrous consequences. It should be emphasised that our goal is to refine, and not to reject economic assumptions and models."

Max Bazerman and Deepak Malhotra (2005)

Economic Rationalism and Public Policy in Singapore

Standard economic theory often starts with the assumption that people are rational, self-interested, utility-maximising agents. This view of human agency — which can be described as economic rationalism — has played a key role in informing public policies. Because individuals are assumed to rationally weigh the costs and benefits of competing options, economic rationalism says that the best way of affecting people's decisions is by altering incentives. As the authors of *Freakonomics*, Steven Levitt and Stephen Dubner, put it, "Economics is at root the study of incentives... Economists love incentives. They love to dream up and enact them, study them and tinker with them. The typical economist believes the world has not yet invented a problem that he cannot fix if given a free hand to design the proper incentive scheme" (Levitt and Dubner 2005, p. 20).

Economists often tell governments to "get incentives right". By tweaking people's assessment of their costs or benefits, incentives allow the policymaker to influence people's decisions in desired and predictable directions. This rationalist paradigm is at the heart of policymaking in governments everywhere — but perhaps nowhere more than in Singapore.

A few examples will suffice to illustrate this. Singapore embraces (almost unilateral) free trade in goods. There are no tariffs on imports and no subsidies for domestic producers. This ensures that domestic producers have every incentive to be as efficient and productive as possible. It also ensures that prices accurately reflect scarcity: they are neither artificially depressed by subsidies nor inflated by tariffs.

In the provision of public services such as healthcare and public housing, the government relies on co-payment to avoid overconsumption and moral hazard, and to ensure that users face the right incentives. It also relies on the price mechanism to force consumers or businesses to take into account the costs they impose on the rest of society. For instance, the government makes extensive use of road pricing so that drivers will internalise the social costs of congestion. At the same time, it imposes high taxes on vehicles and uses an auction system to allocate a limited number of car ownership rights known as Certificates of Entitlement (COEs). The result is a unique system of taxes and cap-and-trade to manage the number of vehicles in Singapore. To manage the demand for foreign workers, the state imposes a levy on employers hiring low-skilled foreign workers. The Goods and Services Tax (GST) is applied uniformly on all goods and services; even "essentials" such as food, healthcare and education are not exempt. This ensures that relative prices are not distorted. To address concerns over social equity and the progressiveness of the fiscal system, the government provides direct cash transfers to lower-income groups in the form of "GST credits". To discourage gambling, the government imposes a levy of S$100 on citizens and permanent residents entering the casinos in Singapore.

This paradigm of economic rationalism has served Singapore well. It has helped to ensure that public policies are mostly efficient even if they are not always popular. By ensuring that price incentives are not muted or distorted, and by letting markets operate with minimal government interference, the government allows markets to work their magic in achieving efficiency. Prices are widely used to reflect the scarcity of resources and to ration demand — not just for privately provided goods and services but also publicly provided ones.

What Behavioural Economics says about Cognition and Choice

Economic rationalism and the tools of standard economics remain an essential part of the policymaker's toolkit. However, although still necessary, they are no longer sufficient as a guide to policymaking. Policymakers have come to recognise that the assumptions of human agency in textbook economics do not always conform to reality. Cognition and choice — how people actually think about the options they face and their conscious or unconscious decision-making processes — turn out to be far more complicated than a cost-benefit calculation. Even if people implicitly undertake a cost-benefit calculation, they are often influenced by a number of psychological and social factors. It behoves the policymaker to better understand what drives people's cognitive and decision-making processes.

In the last three decades, various streams of research from psychology and other social sciences tell us that people are not always the rational, interest-maximising agents described in economics textbooks. In particular, the growing body of research in behavioural economics has consistently shown a number of situations in which individuals act in ways that run counter to the predictions of standard economics.

Mullainathan and Thaler (2000) define behavioural economics as the "combination of psychology and economics that investigates what happens in markets in which some of the agents display human limitations and complications". Behavioural economics tells us that people's rationality, willpower and self-interest are bounded. Individuals have limited computational power which means that instead of applying cost-benefit calculations, they often rely on simple rules of thumb when confronted with complicated decisions, such as those involving risks and probabilities.

Our bounded rationality manifests itself in a number of ways. For instance, we have a status quo bias, which means we are more likely to stick with a position that was set for us than we are to choose it from a menu of choices. This is why more people participate in a retirement savings plan if they are enrolled in it by default than if they are asked to sign up for it. We are also loss averse, which means we value losses more than gains of the same size. How a problem is framed matters too: we are more likely to undergo a medical procedure if we are told that 90% of patients survive than if we are told that 10% die, even though both statements convey identical information. Our utility often depends more on how well we do relative to people around us rather than on absolute measures.

Another stream of behavioural economics highlights our limited self-control or willpower. Left to ourselves, we often do not save enough for retirement even when we have the means to do so. We do not have sufficient health insurance coverage and are unwilling to contemplate bad health outcomes. We often do not buy energy-efficient appliances even though we will save money in the long run. We put off doing the things that will incur short-term costs but reap larger, longer-term benefits — such as quitting smoking, eating more healthily or exercising regularly.

This conflict between our immediate and long-term interests results in inconsistent preferences over time, as well as the tendency to favour instant gratification over future benefits. The comedian, Jerry Seinfeld, understood this human frailty well when he said:

> *I never get enough sleep. I stay up late at night because I'm Night Guy. Night Guy wants to stay up late. 'What about getting up after five hours' sleep?' Oh, that's Morning Guy's problem. That's not my problem. I'm Night Guy — I stay up as late as I want. So you get up in the morning... you're exhausted, you're groggy. 'Oh I hate that Night Guy!' Night Guy always screws Morning Guy. There's nothing Morning Guy can do. The only thing Morning Guy can do is try to oversleep often enough so that Day Guy loses his job and Night Guy has no money to go out anymore.*

Jerry Seinfeld (1993)

On the upside, people are not just self-interested agents: they also have the capacity for generosity and charity, for concern about people not related to them, and for contributing to society without expectation of pay or reward. We also care about fairness and the norms and values of the society in which we live.

These cognitive biases and limitations matter for policy design. Policymakers deal with the real world and are faced with real world problems. While the textbook economic models based on rationality may be internally consistent, policymakers have to grapple with the messiness and complications of the societies they serve. It helps if they have rigorous ways of understanding human motivations and decision-making processes. If so, they are more likely to devise policies that accommodate our human traits and frailties. By taking into account people's cognitive abilities, limitations and biases, behavioural economics offers policymakers the prospect of improving policy design and, thereby, policy outcomes.

So what insight does behavioural economics offer policymakers? For a start, cognitive psychologists have found that we often make irrational or sub-optimal decisions in situations that involve risk and uncertainty, that require us to make trade-offs between present and future consumption, or that entail complicated calculations. Faced with these cognitively challenging tasks, it turns out that our actions cannot always be explained by the rational, cost-benefit calculations that conventional economists are familiar with. Instead, we are often guided by our intuitions, biases, the heuristics or mental shortcuts we apply, the social context (such as social norms), and the way the problem is framed to us. Rather than optimise, we often aim only to "satisfice" — a term coined by Herbert Simon (1956) to describe how people frequently come up with simple and adequate, but not always rational or optimal, solutions to thorny problems.

Behavioural economics brings the findings of psychology to bear in explaining why our decisions or actions often diverge from those of an idealised rational agent. Although the beginnings of behavioural economics can be traced to the work of Herbert Simon in the 1950s, it only received greater attention from mainstream economists after the ground-breaking work of Daniel Kahneman and Amos Tversky in the late 1970s. With the launch of popular books on behavioural economics such as Dan Ariely's *Predictably Irrational* and Richard Thaler and Cass Sunstein's *Nudge* in the last few years, the subject has gained further traction among policymakers attracted by the possibility that behavioural economics offers a way of improving policy design beyond the standard economist's prescription of getting incentives right.

Two Objectives

This book represents the Singapore Civil Service College's efforts to contribute to policymakers' understanding of behavioural economics. It aims to do two things. First, using policy examples from

Singapore, the book tries to explain how behavioural considerations can help to improve the design of public policies. There is broad consensus among scholars of public policy that Singapore's policies reflect the economist's emphasis on efficiency and on getting incentives right. Less well known is how in many instances, policies have also been adjusted to take into account people's biases, decision-making processes and likely (as opposed to theoretical) responses. While Singapore's policymakers may not have been aware of the findings of behavioural economists in academia, they were nonetheless conscious of the need to take into account people's psychology and cognitive limitations when formulating and implementing policies.

Many of the contributions in this volume show that while the government paid a great deal of attention to efficiency considerations, it was also attuned to what might broadly be termed "psychological" considerations. In a number of instances, policymakers tried to take into account people's computational abilities and limitations, their status quo bias (which suggests the use of defaults in which people are automatically enrolled in a programme but have the choice to opt out), their tendency to focus only on their present utility and to heavily discount the future, their aversion to losses, and their assessments of probability based on easily available evidence. The central argument of this book is that public policies in Singapore mostly went with the grain, not just of economic incentives, but also of cognitive psychology.

This is not to suggest that mistakes were not made or that policymakers knew the behaviourally compatible solutions right from the start. In many (if not most) instances, finding the right policy design was a process of experimentation, error and learning-by-doing.

Beyond documentation, this book has a second, more forward-looking purpose — to explore how Singapore's policymakers might apply the insights of behavioural economics more broadly. We hope to generate greater interest and more informed discussion on how behavioural economics can improve policy design and achieve better outcomes.

In a number of areas, the government continues to experiment and to seek improvements to policy design. Behavioural economics can offer a practical guide for effective policy action in a number of policy domains. Take land transport for instance. Encouraging greater use of public transport and less reliance on private transport is not just a matter of economic incentives; it is also a matter of habits and social norms. Promoting environmental sustainability — such as encouraging energy efficient practices, recycling and resource conservation — is another area where there is significant potential to apply the insights of behavioural economics. Not everyone needs to behave in the ways suggested by behavioural economics to make it a useful guide for policymakers. As long as most, or even some, do, that is sufficient. For instance, not everyone needs to change their driving habits to make encouraging some of them to drive at off-peak times a worthwhile thing to do. If behavioural economics can suggest ways in which some motorists might be persuaded to switch to public transport or drive off-peak, it is already a valuable aid to policymakers.

Caveats and Criticisms

Two caveats are in order. First, it bears repeating that we see behavioural economics as augmenting, not supplanting, conventional economics in public policy. By providing another lens to evaluate policy options, behavioural economics provides policymakers an additional set of tools they can apply in policy formulation. In a more complex, multi-faceted and heterogeneous polity, governments can do with more tools to devise creative policy solutions.

Second, just as the student of conventional economics may overreach by insisting on the unbounded rationality of economic agents, so too might the zealous student of behavioural economics overstate the inability of human beings of making any correct decisions at all. The notion of an individual who is so overwhelmed by his cognitive biases and complications as to be incapable of making sensible decisions is as much a caricature as that of a perfectly rational individual. If policymakers begin with such a view of human agency, their response is likely to be far more paternalistic, choice-limiting and heavy-handed than it needs to be. The libertarian paternalism advanced by the behavioural economists Thaler and Sunstein (2003) could easily turn into hard paternalism that eliminates choice altogether.

A related question is why governments should try to help citizens choose wisely at all. Doesn't it smack of paternalism? One answer is that governments often have no choice but to guide people's decisions one way or the other. As Thaler and Sunstein (2008) argue, governments often cannot remain neutral even if they wanted to. Something must serve as the default option; information must be presented one way or another and how the information is presented has an influence ón how people choose. Governments can choose to set the default or frame the information with an idea of which option would benefit most citizens, or they can do so unthinkingly (perhaps randomly) and hope for the best. It is also quite likely that many, if not most, citizens want the authorities to provide some guidance, or at least the relevant information that will help them choose sensibly. This is particularly so when they are confronted with complicated choices: retirement saving plans, health insurance options, medical treatment alternatives, electricity plans, or even the seemingly simple decision of whether to switch from private to public transport. And for those who want to decide without any guidance from the state, behavioural economics does not prescribe restricting their freedom to choose for themselves. For instance, people should still be allowed to opt out of whatever defaults that have been set for them.

Modern society, particularly in the domain of commercially provided goods and services, often presents us with a bewildering array of choices. A visit to any large supermarket should be sufficient to persuade us that the problem faced by affluent societies is not the lack of choice, but a surfeit of it. Behavioural research has shown that increasing the number of choices presented to individuals may not always yield better decisions or improvements in our well-being. As Schwartz (2004) argues, beyond a certain point, "choice no longer liberates, but debilitates". Instead of helping us make better decisions, more choices can lead to confusion, indecision, paralysis, anxiety and regret. This suggests that when government presents citizens with more choices — as it often must to meet more diverse and heterogeneous needs — it should also provide the information and guidance that will help them choose sensibly.

Critics of the application of behavioural economics to policy design sometimes argue that governments have neither the ability to determine what is best for individuals nor the incentives to guide people in making better decisions. This argument is often used by public choice theorists sceptical of the ability or motivation of government officials to improve public outcomes. A related criticism is that government itself may suffer from the same cognitive limitations and biases that cognitive psychologists say afflict individuals. After all, the problems that ordinary folk have trouble computing and dealing rationally with — evaluating short-term costs against long-term benefits, managing risk and uncertainty, and choosing from among a large number of alternatives — are also often the very problems that governments have to grapple with.

There is now a growing body of research to highlight the types of cognitive biases and errors that policymakers and regulators commonly exhibit (Tasic 2010). When assessing risks for instance, policymakers may give undue attention to recent or highly memorable events; this is commonly known as the availability heuristic or the saliency bias in the behavioural economics literature. Like ordinary folk, policymakers too may overestimate the likelihood of events that come easily to mind. For instance, they would assess the environmental costs of nuclear power to be much higher after a nuclear power plant accident even if the underlying risks of an accident have not changed. Faced with uncertainty, policymakers may also exhibit a tendency to overreact — a bias to take action even if this is not (yet) warranted (Patt and Zeckhauser 2000). In an increasingly unpredictable and complex environment — where causal relations often cannot be established *ex ante* — the government's action bias can be a handicap. Conversely, a deeply entrenched bureaucracy may have a strong preference to maintain the status quo, and it may be slow to take action even when these are urgently needed. Yet another cognitive bias is the affect heuristic which Slovic *et al.* (2002) define as the impact of the perceived goodness or badness of intent on our judgement of the act. This means that policymakers arrive at a decision not just by using their reasoning capacities but also by emotions. To put it starkly, if government itself is subject to these biases, why should we assume that it can help citizens make better decisions?

We acknowledge that policymakers also have their own cognitive limitations, biases and blindsides. But the solution to this is not for government to abdicate its responsibility for ensuring good policy design. Instead, the lesson for government is to be cognisant of its vulnerability to biases and to take active steps to correct for them. For instance, to counter status quo bias, it may deliberately bring in external voices to question and critique its prevailing assumptions. It can also deal with increased uncertainty and complexity with tools such as scenario planning and environmental scanning. Done well, these can correct for — or at least moderate — the biases of policymakers. In short, the solution is not for governments to stop doing what they are doing but to find ways to do their job better.

The Chapters

This book is organised in two parts. Part I looks at how policymakers can integrate the growing body of insights from behavioural economics with existing policy design approaches. Chapter 1 reviews the main ideas that have emerged in behavioural economics and how they may complement the Singapore government's policymaking culture of pragmatic rationalism. In particular, it discusses how cognitive psychology has enriched our understanding of people's motivations and cognitive processes. Armed with these insights, policymakers can design policies that better accommodate our cognitive limits and biases. Chapter 2 takes a different tack. Focusing on the *external* constraints that social norms may impose on individual decisions, it explores how norms may interact with economic incentives and how governments can harness both to achieve their policy goals.

Part II of the book looks at how the Singapore government has applied — and could apply — the insights of behavioural economics in various policy domains. Chapter 3 describes Singapore's experience in using behavioural economics to tackle the urban blight of traffic congestion. Chapter 4 discusses how the concepts of behavioural economics can be intelligently applied to promote environmentally friendly behaviours. Chapter 5 explores how behavioural economics can help energy regulators promote competition in electricity retail.

Chapter 6 takes a macroeconomic tack: it examines how discretionary fiscal transfers can be better designed by taking into account heuristics such as anchoring, discounting, framing and mental accounting. Chapter 7 looks at how economics thinking has shaped Singapore's public healthcare policies and explores how behavioural economics can improve policy design and help Singaporeans make better health decisions. Chapter 8 discusses CPF LIFE — Singapore's recently introduced national annuity scheme. It examines how the Singapore government responded to the public's concerns by adjusting and communicating the key parameters of the annuity scheme in a way that was consistent with ideas from behavioural economics.

Finally, Chapter 9 surveys the major findings in behavioural economics that can be used in a number of policy areas. In particular, it highlights the findings which are relatively unexplored and less well-understood in terms of their application to policy design and regulatory reform.

Governments are beginning to take seriously the insights and practical ideas of behavioural economics, Singapore's is no exception. This book is a modest contribution of the Singapore government's experience in applying behavioural economics in various policy areas. We hope that it makes a useful addition to the ongoing discourse and that our readers will be encouraged to further consider and question how public policies can be improved by taking account of people's psychology.

References

Bazerman, Max and Deepak Malhotra (2005). "Economics Wins, Psychology Loses, and Society Pays." *Harvard NOM Working Paper*, No. 05–07.

Levitt, Steven and Stephen Dubner (2005). *Freakonomics: A Rogue Economist Explores the Hidden Side of Everything*. William Morrow/ HarperCollins.

Lunn, Pete (2008). "Behavioural Economics: Is it such a Big Deal?" *Prospect Magazine*, Issue 150, September 2008, viewed 3 January 2011, http://www.prospectmagazine.co.uk/2008/09/behavioural economicsisitsuchabigdeal/

Mullainathan, Sendhil and Richard Thaler (2000). "Behavioural Economics." *NBER Working Paper* 7948, National Bureau of Economic Research.

Patt, Anthony and Richard Zeckhauser (2000). "Action Bias and Environmental Decisions." *Journal of Risk and Uncertainty*, Vol. 21, No. 1, pp. 45–72.

Schwartz, Barry (2004). *The Paradox of Choice: Why More is Less*. Harper Perennial.

Seinfeld, Jerry (1993). "The Glasses." *Seinfeld*, Season 5, Episode 3.

Simon, Herbert (1956). "Rational Choice and the Structure of the Environment." *Psychological Review*, Vol. 63, No. 2, pp. 129–138.

Slovic, Paul, Melissa Finucane, Ellen Peters and Donald MacGregor (2002). "The Affect Heuristic," in Thomas Gilovich, Dale Griffin and Daniel Kahneman, eds., *Heuristics and Biases: The Psychology of Intuitive Judgement*. Cambridge University Press.

Tasic, Slavisa (2010). "Are Regulators Rational?" *7th Mises Seminar*, Istituto Bruno Leoni, 9–10 October.

Thaler, Richard and Cass Sunstein (2003). "Libertarian Paternalism." *American Economics Review*, Vol. 93, No. 2, pp. 175–179.

Thaler, Richard and Cass Sunstein (2008). *Nudge: Improving Decisions About Health, Wealth and Happiness*. Yale University Press.

The Economist (1999). "Rethinking Thinking." 16 December, viewed 3 January 2011, http://www.economist.com

PART I

CHAPTER 1

KEY IDEAS IN BEHAVIOURAL ECONOMICS — AND WHAT THEY MEAN FOR POLICY DESIGN

KOH Tsin Yen

Introduction

A primary function of policymakers is to anticipate the impact of their policies and assess the likelihood that their policies will yield the desired outcomes. Will lowering income tax rates increase investment by firms and encourage more work by individuals, or will it leave firm and worker behaviour unchanged? Will raising road usage charges lead to a decline in the number of cars on the road or will it have no impact on driver behaviour? Will increasing maternity benefits result in an increase in fertility rates, or will it simply become deadweight funding for the state? At the heart of these and many other policy decisions are implicit assumptions and questions about the factors which drive human decisions and behaviour.

The dominant theory of decision making in economics and other social sciences has been the rational choice model. People are generally assumed to be self-interested, rational agents: they analyse the costs and benefits of various options and choose the option that maximises their utility. They have stable, consistent preferences and the options they face are comparable to one another. This model is also a common paradigm for analysing policy decisions. In choosing between various options, policymakers typically assume that people will respond rationally — and therefore predictably — to incentives. Consequently, the right policy is that which creates incentives for the desired behaviour.

In the last thirty years or so, behavioural economics has emerged as a way of introducing insights from psychology into economics. Behavioural economics starts from the observation, borne out by numerous experiments, that individuals often deviate from strict rationality in systematic ways, not just arbitrarily or occasionally. This field of economics seeks to introduce more robust and realistic descriptive models of decision making and choice into standard economic theory. The implications of behavioural economics have not been lost on policymakers, and attention to the field has grown in academic and policy communities.

Individuals often deviate from strict rationality in systematic ways, not just arbitrarily or occasionally.

This chapter will first describe how economic theory, and in particular the rational choice model, has been applied in Singapore's public policy context. It then explains the challenge behavioural economics poses to the rational choice model, finally concluding with the implications of behavioural economics for public policy, particularly in Singapore's context.

The Economic Foundations of Public Policy in Singapore

The Singapore government prides itself on its pragmatic and rational approach to public policy. Prime Minister Lee Hsien Loong once described Singaporean civil servants as "practis[ing] public administration almost in laboratory conditions", referring to the environment that supports, "Singapore's ability to take a longer view, pursue rational policies, put in place the fundamentals which the country needs, and systematically change policies which are outdated or obsolete" (Lee 2005, p. 7). One manifestation of this rationality in government is in the application of economic principles to almost all areas of public policy.

There are at least three main ways in which this is done. The first and most obvious is in the use of incentives to shape or change behaviour. People and firms are assumed to respond rationally to incentives. Lowering corporate tax rates will lead to higher levels of private investment, raising road usage charges will lead to fewer cars on the road, and increasing maternity and other parenthood benefits will result in an increase in birth rates. Getting incentives right is arguably one of the most important considerations in the design and implementation of public policy in Singapore. For instance, while the government subsidises healthcare expenses, it also requires that users co-pay a share of their medical bills. The primary consideration behind this policy is the concern that free healthcare will erode the incentive for users to exercise prudence and economise in their healthcare consumption decisions. Co-payment is seen as necessary to align the incentives of the patient and the payer (in this case, the government), and limit people's propensity to over-consume publicly subsidised services.

Another area in which public policy decisions are motivated largely by the incentive effects they produce is in the design of welfare policy. Singapore has always resisted the introduction of a universal, needs-based welfare system because of the adverse incentive effects and moral hazard problems that such a system would generate. Raising the benefits of being unemployed, it is argued, would lower the cost of unemployment for the individual and result in more people choosing to remain unemployed. Instead, Singapore's approach is to "make work pay" through wage supplementation for low-wage workers.

The second way in which the Singapore government applies conventional economics in public policy is in the use of cost-benefit analysis. The rational choice model assumes that agents are able to generate a range of alternatives and to weigh the costs and benefits of each alternative before deciding on a course of action. As a theory of decision making for individuals, it has been criticised on both descriptive and normative grounds. As a theory of public decision making, however, it is not inaccurate. Cost-benefit analysis is an indispensable part of the Singapore policymaker's toolkit. Should the government build a new subway line? Should it finance the development of a high-speed fibre optic network? Will casinos bring greater benefits to Singapore than the social costs that might be created? No matter the policy domain, the policymaker is expected to generate a range of alternatives and make an objective assessment of the costs and benefits of the various alternatives, before arriving at a decision. Cost-benefit analysis, while imperfect and dependent on the assumptions made by policymakers, at least attempts to provide an objective basis on which to assess the relative merits of different options.

More broadly, the crux of policymaking lies in balancing and making trade-offs between competing values and priorities. Not all costs and benefits are easily quantifiable or commensurable — it is not immediately obvious, for example, how one might assess whether a plot of land should be set aside for a church, a school or an office building — but the process of cost-benefit analysis forces the policymaker to explicitly and deliberately consider the trade-offs that need to be made and to attempt to put the competing demands on a common metric.

A third way in which standard microeconomic principles are applied in Singapore public policy is in the area of market liberalisation and regulation. This involves considerations such as the structure of the market that best promotes competition, the pace of liberalisation, and the regulation of any remaining monopoly power post-liberalisation. With a relatively small domestic market, economies of scale and scope make it likely that the outcome of liberalisation would be monopolies or oligopolies in areas such as the provision of potable water, the electricity grid and public transport. The overriding concern for regulators would then be to prevent firms or entities with monopolistic power from abusing their market power, while not eroding incentives for them to improve their performance.

In each of these examples, the principle of the Singapore government has been to work with incentives and make use of markets even when it accepts the need for some form of government intervention. Policies are designed to align or strengthen the incentives to produce particular outcomes, rather than to mandate outcomes.

Bounded Rationality, Bounded Self-Control, Bounded Self-Interest

The influence of neoclassical economics policymaking in Singapore has been significant but not exclusive. Experienced policymakers, whether in Singapore or elsewhere, know that people do not always act rationally or in a way consistent with their long-term interests. This could be for any number of reasons — they may not be able to assess the costs and benefits of various options accurately, or it may be too complicated for them to do so; they may not have the willpower or self-control to act in their own interests; they may make seemingly sub-optimal choices for reasons not adequately acknowledged by the rational choice model, such as altruism; or their decisions may be shaped by heuristics and cognitive biases. The reality is that policymakers have to consider how people *actually* make decisions — as opposed to how textbook economics assumes they will make decisions — when designing and implementing policies.

This is where the behavioural sciences have made a valuable contribution to our understanding of decision making. We can understand the development of behavioural economics and its acceptance into mainstream economics as book-ended by two Nobel Prizes in Economics, notable for their being awarded not to economists but to psychologists. The first Nobel Prize was given to Herbert Simon in 1978 for his work in developing the concept of bounded rationality. Simon argued that the theory of rational choice favoured by classical economic theory placed unrealistically high cognitive demands on people — it was simply not possible for individuals and firms to generate all possible alternatives, or to work out the consequences of the full range of alternatives, or even to adjudicate between competing wants (especially by equating costs and benefits at the margin). Instead, Simon proposed that a descriptive theory of decision making should replace the concept of utility maximisation. He called it "satisficing" — the notion that economic agents generated an aspiration of the kind of solution they were looking for, searched for it one solution at a time, and stopped searching once they had found something acceptably close to their aspiration. Aspirations were not static but could change as people accumulated experience (Simon 1979).

The second prize was awarded to the psychologist Daniel Kahneman in 2002. Kahneman and his main collaborator, the late Amos Tversky, built on Simon's work to draw "maps of bounded rationality" by exploring the differences between the choices people actually made under conditions of uncertainty and the choices predicted by the rational choice model (Kahneman 2002).

Each of the three lines explored by Kahneman and Tversky — heuristics and biases, prospect theory and loss aversion, and framing effects — has had significant implications for economics. For example, the idea that people are generally loss averse, a central proposition of prospect theory, has led to the exploration of what behavioural economists call the endowment effect, or the value we place on our possessions solely because they belong to us

(Kahneman and Tversky 1979). The endowment effect has been documented in now-famous experiments with mugs and chocolate of equivalent value: undergraduates doubled the value of the mug or chocolate they had after it was given to them (Kahneman *et al.* 1990).

In the same vein, behavioural economist Dan Ariely (2008) found that students at Duke University were willing to pay about $170 to buy basketball tickets on the black market but demanded $2,400 if the tickets were in their possession. In other words, the mere fact of possession added $2,230 to the value ascribed to the ticket. The endowment effect can also be used to explain why willingness-to-accept surveys generally produce higher values than willingness-to-pay surveys for things as diverse as postal service, trees and goose hunting permits (Kahneman *et al.* 1990). Clearly, the endowment effect and the consequent difference between willingness-to-accept and willingness-to-pay prices defy the law of one price assumed in standard economics. It also raises the question of how policymakers should assess costs and benefits.

Yet another twist to standard cost-benefit analysis is the idea of mental accounting, which can be understood as a heuristic people use to simplify complicated and uncertain decisions. The theory is that we assign our expenditures to specific categories or mental accounts, such as housing, food, leisure and so on, and we balance costs and benefits on an account basis, rather than an overall basis (Thaler 1999). Mental accounting and loss aversion together can result in sub-optimal decisions, as illustrated by a study of New York taxi drivers. New York taxi drivers pay a fixed rental fee for their taxis and keep all the money they earn from driving passengers. They can decide how long they want to drive each day. A study by Colin Camerer and his collaborators found that taxi drivers had an idea of how much they needed to earn per day and would work until they reached that point — meaning that they stopped early on good days, e.g. rainy days or when a convention was in town, and they stopped later on bad days, whereas the optimal strategy would be to work more on good days and cut their losses on bad days (Camerer *et al.* 1997).

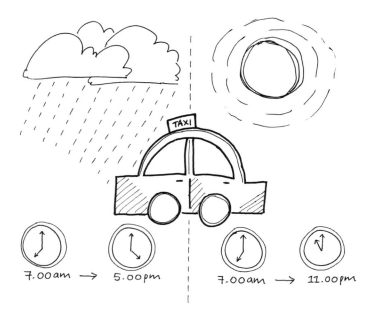

Economists have also explored other bounds in "the inner environment of the mind", as Simon puts it (since the bounds in the external environment were well known to economists), apart from bounds on rational thought and their implications for economic theory. In their introduction to behavioural economics, Thaler and Mullainathan identified two other bounds on rational action of particular interest to economists: bounded self-control and bounded selfishness (Mullainathan and Thaler 2000).

One manifestation of bounded self-control could be status quo bias or the tendency to stick with the current situation, either out of fear of the devil you don't know (arguably a manifestation of loss aversion) or, less charitably, laziness and procrastination. Another example of bounded self-control can be found in the area of savings. The life-cycle hypothesis suggests that we should smoothen income and consumption over our life-cycle — if we expect to earn most of our income when we are young, we should save more now, in anticipation of our old age. In practice, our consumption tracks income more closely than predicted by the life-cycle hypothesis (Mullainathan and Thaler 2000). One reason could be because of hyperbolic discount rates, leading us to heavily discount (or put a lot less value on) future utility more than a rational being would (Thaler and Shefrin 1981). Another could simply be a lack of self-control, or the gap between how much we think we should save and how much we do save. Imperfect self-control, and the knowledge of that imperfection, could explain the popularity of save-as-you-earn programmes despite their low interest returns. These programmes allow participants to make binding commitments to save a particular percentage of their pay every month, in effect imposing external constraints on their present selves for the sake of their future selves.

In an example of how policies can be designed to take advantage of insights from behavioural economics, Thaler teamed up with economist Shlomo Benartzi on the design of the Save More Tomorrow scheme. The problem they sought to address was the low take-up of corporate savings plans, even though many companies offered their employees incentives to participate in these plans. To counter hyperbolic discounting and loss aversion, the Save More Tomorrow scheme allowed participants to commit a percentage of their future income increases, e.g. from promotions and bonuses, rather than present income, towards their savings plan. Take-up rates for the scheme increased dramatically, as did savings (Benartzi and Thaler 2004). Thaler and Benartzi's scheme demonstrates the value of behavioural economics for public policy — it can help to improve policy design and make it more likely for people to choose particular actions or behaviour (in this case, saving for one's own retirement) without overly circumscribing their choices.

The third bound identified by Thaler and Mullanaithan is "bounded selfishness". Economic theory does not require the baker, the butcher or the candlestick maker to be selfish, though many economic theorems and problems are based on this premise (the tragedy of the commons and other failures of collective action, for example). There is increasing recognition that economic theory requires a "thicker" description of economic behaviour than that of rational choice. One example is in the growth of literature on the importance of institutions in enabling, stabilising, regulating and legitimising markets.[1] Behavioural economists also argue that economic theory should consider the social context that informs and shapes individual decisions, such as social and cultural norms.

One such norm could be fairness. Repeated experiments with the ultimatum game, for example, suggest that fairness acts as a constraint in strategic considerations of self-interest in two ways: proposers tend to make higher offers than predicted by perfect sub-game equilibrium (which is an offer just above zero), and responders tend to reject offers they deem too insultingly low (typically anything less than 20% of whatever is at stake) even though this comes at a cost to themselves.[2] Playing the game in small-scale societies (e.g. small farming and village communities in Africa and South America) instead of undergraduate classrooms yields similar results — the higher the degree of market integration and the higher the payoffs to cooperation in that society, the greater the level of cooperation in the ultimatum game (Heinrich *et al.* 2001). Another social and cultural norm could be repugnance, which arises in connection with items like human organs or babies where markets could, and arguably need to, be established but are not because the idea of buying and selling these as commodities is repugnant to most people (Roth 2007).

Not only do social norms inform behaviour, our response to the same situation may also change depending on whether it is

---

[1] For example, see Rodrik and Subramanian (2003).

[2] In Mullainathan and Thaler (2000), the ultimatum game is played between two people, a proposer and a responder. The proposer is asked to divide a sum of money in any way between him and the responder. The responder is asked if he would accept the allocation. If the responder agrees, the sum is divided as proposed; if the responder disagrees, neither receives any money. There could be an endowment effect here, since $10 (for example) forgone is not valued as much as actually handing over $10 of one's own money.

governed by social norms or market norms. In *Predictably Irrational,* for example, Dan Ariely (2008) offers an illustration. Some lawyers, when approached by the American Association for Retired People (AARP), declined to offer their services to needy retirees at a discounted rate (of $30 an hour, for example) but overwhelmingly agreed to provide the same services for free. This suggested to Ariely that seeking to replace social norms with market norms could come at a cost.

We could make the broader point that how a policy is framed and presented to the public can have a significant impact on how it is received. In his classic work on collective action, Mancur Olson (1971) distinguished between logics of consequences (preached and followed by the rational agent model) and logics of appropriateness. Policymakers may have better success in their policy outcomes if they can influence the way the problem is framed. For example, a tax law professor at Cardozo Law School in New York City, Edward Zelinsky, explored framing effects in the analysis of tax expenditure (Zelinsky 2005). Zelinsky conducted a survey to explore public perceptions of compensation for volunteer firemen. A small number of respondents (10–20%, depending on how the survey was designed and the amount of compensation) thought

that giving cash would compromise the firemen's volunteer status while giving an economically equivalent amount through the tax system would not, suggesting that their responses were affected by the way in which the compensation was framed. This conclusion could be generalised to tax expenditures: tax expenditures are often designed to be equivalent to direct cash outlays, but are nonetheless viewed differently from cash outlays — less like cash than cash — which might explain the occasional preference of legislators for tax breaks over cash grants.

Public Policy Implications and Applications

The preceding section outlines several of the key ideas that have emerged from behavioural economics and some of their implications for public policy. One clear implication is that the way in which a policy is designed and implemented can affect its outcome. In *Nudge*, an influential book on behavioural economics and public policy, Thaler and Sunstein (2008) argue that since all problems and policies have to be framed in some way, governments should take seriously the idea of choice architecture and seek to structure their policies in ways that nudge people towards the better choices (in the government's best judgement, at any rate).[3]

We can identify at least three behavioural economic lessons for policymakers. The first is that for any number of reasons — loss aversion, status quo bias, endowment effects, inertia, hyperbolic discounting or sheer laziness — people often stick to the status quo, even if their rational minds know that a change would better serve their interests. This is why defaults and opt-out clauses are important components of any policymaker's tool kit. Examples of the use of defaults in Singapore include organ donations (under the Human Organ Transplant Act, individuals are presumed to have given their consent to donate their organs upon their death unless they have opted out of donation) and participation in MediShield, Singapore's national catastrophic illness insurance programme.

Second, we can think about defaults as part of a broader point about how choices should be structured. The behavioural economics literature suggests that people often make systematic and predictable errors when faced with decisions involving risk and uncertainty. Defaults are one way to structure complex choices to help people avoid error and make better decisions. Another way could be to provide more salient information, such as on energy consumption by household appliances, to persuade people into making better decisions (Thaler and Sunstein 2008). The story of

---

[3] This is their list of policy design principles: getting incentives right, understanding mappings, e.g. from products to money; setting appropriate defaults; giving feedback; expecting error and designing policies that can accept a certain amount of human error; and structuring complex choices. These approaches to policy design can help governments nudge people in the right directions while preserving their freedom to choose a different option from that suggested by the authorities.

how CPF LIFE, Singapore's national longevity insurance scheme, was introduced suggests that policymakers can help people make better decisions by simplifying otherwise complicated choices, including the possibility of *reducing* the number of options that are offered to them.

Third, and arguably most importantly, how choices are framed matters. If people often choose based on the most salient or accessible features of the situation rather than an objective and exhaustive cost-benefit analysis of their options, then framing the situation differently can induce different choices. The way a policy is presented can bring to mind particular emotions or associations or norms (logics of appropriateness) and thus trigger particular actions or behaviours.

An illustration of framing effects is organ donation. In Singapore, the gap between the supply and demand of organs is large. Standard economic theory prescribes the free market as the most efficient way to allocate supply to demand. However, there are moral and ethical concerns with organ trading. Apart from the repugnance that society might feel towards the unbridled selling and buying of organs (Roth 2007), there are concerns with the exploitation of sellers, who are likely to be poor, and the diminution of the dignity of human life.[4]

The government framed the issue of payment for organ donors not as a hard-edged economic transaction, but as one of fairness for the donor. In its public consultation exercise, the Ministry of Health (MOH) explained that the proposed legislative amendments were intended to "compensate living donors according to international ethical practices" (MOH 2008b, p. 1). MOH emphasised the distinction between "compensation" and "the buying and selling of organs", with stiffer penalties proposed for the latter. Feedback on

---

[4] As the Minister for Health in 2008, Khaw Boon Wan explained in a reply to a parliamentary question on organ trading on 21 July, "the academic ethicists and medical doctors may be against the sale of organs, but the economists have analysed the problem from a practical perspective, which deserves to be considered." (MOH 2008a, p. 6).

the amendments was generally positive, but some had reservations on the use of "compensation", which could be misunderstood for payment for the organ. By the Second Reading of the Human Organ Transplant (Amendment) Bill, MOH had dropped "compensation" in favour of language that proposed "to reimburse or defray the costs or expenses of living organ donors" (Khaw 2009, p. 2). The Amendment Bill was passed in March 2009.

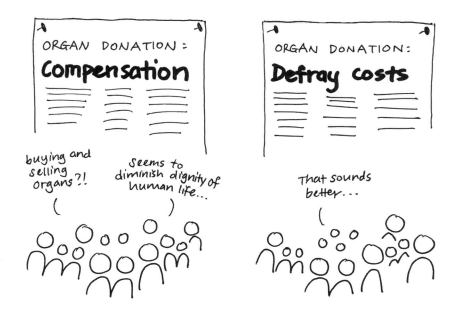

Conclusion

These points on the use of defaults to take advantage of the status quo bias, the need to structure and simplify complex choices, and the importance of framing effects are not new to Singapore policymakers who have always grappled with the psychological elements of public policy. Nonetheless, the dominant model of behaviour is often assumed to be the rational choice model, and policy practitioners in Singapore are more likely to emphasise cost-benefit analyses and getting incentives right, than to account for human foibles, cognitive biases and social norms. This is why the emergence of behavioural economics as a formal discipline is a welcome development. It provides an empirically robust and theoretically sound basis for them to take into account people's likely responses to policies and to consider how policies can be improved by adjusting for people's biases and society's norms.

References

Ariely, Dan (2008). *Predictably Irrational: The Hidden Forces That Shape Our Decisions*. HarperCollins.

Camerer, Colin, Linda Babcock, George Loewenstein and Richard Thaler (1997). "Labor Supply of New York City Cabdrivers: One Day At A Time." *The Quarterly Journal of Economics*, Vol. 112, No. 2, pp. 407–441.

Heinrich, Joseph, Robery Boyd, Samuel Bowles, Colin Camerer, Ernst Fehr, Herbert Gintis and Richard McElreath (2001). "In Search of Homo Economicus: Behavioral Experiments in 15 Small-Scale Societies." *The American Economic Review*, Vol. 91, No. 2, pp. 73–78.

Kahneman, Daniel (2002). "Maps of Bounded Rationality: A Perspective on Intuitive Judgement and Choice", prize lecture, 8 December, viewed 10 May 2010, http://nobelprize.org/nobel_prizes/economics/laureates/2002/kahnemann-lecture.pdf

Kahneman, Daniel, Jack Knetsch and Richard Thaler (1990). "Experimental Tests of the Endowment Effect and the Coase Theorem." *Journal of Political Economy*, Vol. 98, No. 6, pp. 1325–1348.

Kahneman, Daniel and Amos Tversky (1979). "Prospect Theory: An Analysis of Decision under Risk." *Econometrica*, Vol. 47, No. 2, pp. 263–292.

Khaw, Boon Wan (2009). "The Human Organ Transplant (Amendment) Bill Second Reading Speech", 23 March 2009, viewed 20 May 2010, http://www.moh.gov.sg/mohcorp/speeches.aspx?id=21280

Lee, Hsien Loong (2005). "Speech by Prime Minister Lee Hsien Loong at the 2005 Administrative Service Dinner", 24 March 2005, viewed 20 May 2010, http://app.psd.gov.sg/data/SpeechatAdminService Dinner2005-final.pdf

Ministry of Health, Singapore (2008a). "Parliamentary Question on Organ Trading and Transplant", 21 July 2008, viewed 20 May 2010, http://www.moh.gov.sg/mohcorp/parliamentaryqa.aspx?id=19598

Ministry of Health, Singapore (2008b). "MOH Seeks Public Feedback On Proposed Amendments To The Human Organ Transplant Act", press release, 14 November, viewed 20 May 2010, http://www.moh.gov.sg/mohcorp/pressreleases.aspx?id=20320

Mullainathan, Sendhil and Richard Thaler (2000). "Behavioral Economics." *NBER Working Paper* 7848, National Bureau of Economic Research.

Olson, Mancur (1971). *The Logic of Collective Action: Public Goods and the Theory of Groups.* Harvard University Press.

Rodrik, Dani and Arvind Subramanian (2003). "The Primacy of Institutions (And What This Does and Does Not Mean)." *Finance and Development,* June, pp. 31–35.

Roth, Alvin (2007). "Repugnance as a Constraint on Markets." *Journal of Economic Perspectives,* Vol. 21, No. 3, pp. 37–58.

Simon, Herbert (1979). "Rational Decision Making in Business Organizations." *The American Economic Review,* Vol. 69, No. 4, pp. 493–513.

Thaler, Richard (1999). "Mental Accounting Matters." *Journal of Behavioral Decision Making,* Vol. 12, No. 3, pp. 183–206.

Thaler, Richard and Hersh Shefrin (1981). "An Economic Theory of Self-Control." *Journal of Political Economy,* Vol. 89, No. 2, pp. 392–406.

Thaler, Richard and Shlomo Benartzi (2004). "Save More Tomorrow: Using Behavioral Economics to Increase Employee Saving." *Journal of Political Economy,* Vol. 112, No. 1, pp. 164–187.

Thaler, Richard and Cass Sunstein (2008). *Nudge: Improving Decisions about Health, Wealth, and Happiness.* Yale University Press.

Zelinsky, Edward (2005). "Do Tax Expenditures Create Framing Effects? Volunteer Firefighters, Property Tax Exemptions, and the Paradox of Tax Expenditure Analysis." *Virginia Tax Review,* Vol. 24, pp. 797–798.

CHAPTER 2

INCENTIVES, NORMS AND PUBLIC POLICY

Charmaine TAN and Donald LOW

"You might be an economist if you refuse to sell your children because you think they'll be worth more later."

Yoram Bauman (2009)

Introduction

Economists are not known for their sense of humour. Nonetheless, readers may appreciate Bauman's joke for at least two reasons. First, economists are always weighing costs against benefits, often over different time horizons. Second, economists are so adept at reducing everything to prices and monetary incentives that other factors, such as social norms and values, do not seem to figure at all in their explanations of human motivations and behaviours.

A typical starting point in conventional economic theory is that the rational, self-interested individual seeks to maximise his utility, given a set of constraints. In this model, the agent's behaviour is motivated primarily by the economic incentives that he faces. By implication, the way to achieve desired outcomes is to set the right incentives. Therefore, if the task is to induce consumption of "X", an economist's instinctive approach is to reach for the fiscal wallet and hand out cash subsidies or vouchers for "X". In the conventional economic account, social considerations such as norms and values are dismissed as ambiguous, vague and unpredictable, and they are therefore given short shrift. At best, they are treated as an exogenous factor, not as a parameter that policy can alter.

However, theoretical and empirical advances in the field of behavioural economics call for a rethink of how economic incentives determine individual choice when social norms come into play. The findings suggest that far from treating these norms and values as given, policymakers ought to think about how norms might work in tandem or at cross purposes with economic incentives. Behavioural economists have gone further to challenge the long-held assumption that individuals always respond in a rational, interest-maximising way to incentives. As we shall see, introducing a social element into economic theory enriches our understanding of real-world outcomes, yet the role of social norms has not been satisfactorily taken into account in standard economics.

This chapter explores two levels in which social norms may drive a wedge between real-world behaviours and the predictions of standard economics. We first examine how social norms can shape behaviour by operating as "psychological" taxes (in the form of shame or social disapprobation) or subsidies (in the form of social approval). Seen from this perspective, the rational or interest-maximising choice is very much a function of the social context. Furthermore, because individuals need to coordinate their actions to change social norms, a collective action problem often hinders societies from shifting norms in desirable directions. Such problems will be familiar to economists as a type of failure caused by externalities or as a tragedy of the commons, where individually rational actions are not collectively rational.

Second, we consider how social norms may exist as a separate set of rules governing human behaviour. That is, rather than seek to maximise his interests, a person may rely on his value system as the basis for behaviour or decision in some situations. Some examples include social exchanges (say with our kith and kin), organ donations, environmental protection, and philanthropic giving. In such areas, introducing monetary payments as incentives may be deemed as "crossing the line" between social and market norms, and they may turn out to be ineffective or even counter-productive in inducing the desired behavioural change, because they erode or crowd out the very norms or values that sustain the desired behaviour.

Social Forces in Markets and the Collective Action Problem

In his paper "Social Norms and Social Roles", Sunstein (1996) offers a useful three-part framework to consider how social norms influence choices: (i) intrinsic value, (ii) reputational value, and (iii) effect on self-image. To illustrate, you may choose to read a certain book because you find it interesting, pleasant, fun, or illuminating — this is the intrinsic value you derive from the activity. You may also do it because there are reputational advantages, or because you like to think of yourself as the type who appreciates such genre of books. The three motivations might not operate independently of one another. How much reading that book raises your self-perception is very much related to how much admiration it generates in others, which may in turn affect the degree of revelation you gain, or expect to gain from the book. Nonetheless, it is a useful framework to think about the workings through which social norms influence behaviour.

A theory of choice that takes into account both the monetary costs and benefits of an action, as well as those arising from acting with or against socially accepted norms, is not merely a more informed or complete one. It also suggests important implications for policymakers on how desired policy outcomes can be achieved more effectively. Consider the case of tax compliance. If we started off in a world devoid of social norms and sanctions, the expected price to pay for tax evasion, determined by the amount of penalty and the probability of getting caught, would suggest a level of evasion that is higher than actually observed. This suggests that what explains compliance of tax laws is not just its enforcement, but also society's tax-paying norms that people abide by (see for example, Alm *et al.* 1999 and Posner 2000).

In a similar vein, law enforcement alone does not completely explain other behaviours such as non-littering. In today's

Singapore for instance, if one considers only the financial penalty and the probability of being caught littering, the individual may well find littering a rational course of action as the expected penalty of doing so is trivial. When people refrain from littering, the possibility of an environment officer lurking nearby and catching them in the act probably does not come to mind at all. Rather, what stops them from littering is the disapproval from others as well as the intrinsic sense of responsibility they feel towards the society (recall Sunstein's three-part framework), shaped by years of socialisation in a country where littering is widely frowned upon. Economic incentives and social attitudes therefore work in tandem to bring about behavioural change.

Another recent example of how social norms have turned out to be an effective way of influencing behaviour is the notable shift in norms against smoking in Singapore. For many years, the government's efforts to discourage smoking centred on raising tobacco duties. There were however limits to this approach, not least because people's decision to smoke is often determined by social influences rather than a calculation of costs and benefits. If smokers were indeed concerned only with personal costs and benefits of smoking, they would not have engaged in the self-harming behaviour to begin with. Increasing the prices of cigarettes may not be all that effective in lowering the incidence of smoking, i.e. the price elasticity of smoking is relatively low.

This suggests that policies to discourage smoking need to move beyond price incentives, to also focus on changing social norms. When fewer people in the target society are seen smoking, it is easier to convince people that smoking is harmful and for smokers to acknowledge it. With fewer smokers, it is also less likely that people would be influenced to pick it up in a bid to gain social recognition. If smokers are perceived in a negative light, then social forces will start to push in the direction against smoking. For these reasons, the Singapore government has, in recent years, quite aggressively extended the prohibition against smoking to almost all public spaces, to nudge society's norms towards being against smoking.

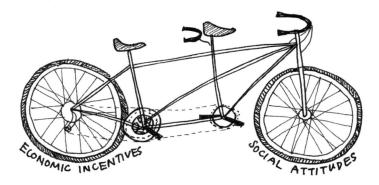

ECONOMIC INCENTIVES

SOCIAL ATTITUDES

Economic incentives and social attitudes work in tandem to bring about behavioural change.

While social norms usually take longer than price incentives to adjust (and the effectiveness of measures to change social norms may be harder to predict), the results from changing norms are likely to be more long-lasting than if only price incentives were changed. Governments — probably more so in Singapore's context — often play a large part in shaping social norms, whether intentionally or not. Policymakers should be aware of how their policies can induce desirable or detrimental shifts in norms. Furthermore, the case for government action is strong given that without intervention, desirable shifts in norms are often impeded by a collective action problem.

To illustrate the problem of collective action, consider how in the past putting on the seat belt in a car was uncommon in many places. If passengers buckled up, it was even considered an insult to the driver (Lessig 1995). The shaming effects associated with buckling up constituted a cost and even the more risk-averse who otherwise might have wanted to buckle up were compelled not to do so. Without coordination, it is difficult for individuals to engineer a shift in norms on wearing seat belts. In the same spirit as that of a prisoner's dilemma, people are doomed to remain in the sub-optimal outcome. That is, in a case where the norm is against wearing seat belts, an individual would choose to "go with the flow" and not buckle up after accounting for the (psychological) cost of doing so, even though he would be better off if the norm allows him to unabashedly put the seat belt on. One of the ways to overcome the problem is for the government to foreclose the least favourable outcome through legislation. With a mandatory seat belt law, the shame put on people who buckle their seat belts is substantially decreased. Over time, putting on the seat belt becomes the norm, and this new norm affects people's underlying preference in the direction of wearing seat belts. Even if the law is not actively enforced, compliance is high.

In this particular example, the degree of government action — legislation — is taken to the extreme. But it need not always be so. Whether social norms are better shaped through education, persuasion, economic incentives or regulations depends on the particular context. Policymakers need to develop a deeper understanding of the role of social norms and the presence of collective action problems, in order to design policies that are effective in the long run.

Social Norms versus Market Incentives

The preceding section discussed how we can integrate social norms into an analytical framework (cost-benefit analysis) that economists are familiar with. Till this point, the basic economic approach in explaining choice has stayed intact. The prescriptions of imposing a penalty (broadly defined to include social disapproval) to discourage an action and a reward (broadly defined to include social approval) to encourage an action are still unchallenged. What we did was to extend conventional rational choice theory based only on financial incentives to take into account the psychological costs or benefits of going against or conforming with social norms. However, one can easily think of many other social interactions where even this "extended version" of rational choice theory fails to satisfactorily account for behaviours.

In his book *The Gift of Relationship: From Blood Donations to Social Policy*, Richard Titmuss (1971) argued that introducing payment for blood donations reduces people's willingness to donate blood because it undermines the inherent social motivations for blood donors. Titmuss also compared the US system with the UK system of blood donations and found that the commercialisation of blood in the former led to shortages and a greater incidence of contaminated blood. While controversial, Titmuss' argument that monetary rewards might sometimes reduce, rather than induce, more supply has attracted much attention.

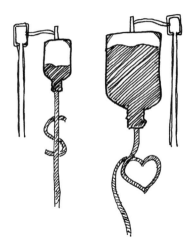

Introducing payment for blood donations reduces people's willingness to donate blood because it undermines the inherent social motivations for blood donors.

Behavioural economics terms this phenomenon the crowding out effect. The underlying behavioural explanation is that humans live simultaneously in two worlds — the market world and the social world. As Dan Ariely (2008) illustrates in *Predictably Irrational*, if you offered to pay your mother-in-law for hosting you to a Thanksgiving dinner, or if you so much as hint to your romantic partner how much you have paid for dinner in expectation of sexual favours, you can expect outrage from them. This is so because exchanges in the world of social relationships are very different from those in markets and are governed by different principles. Moreover, once market norms are introduced into social exchanges, it is often the former which become dominant. It is also subsequently hard to re-establish social relationships even when the market incentives are removed.

Quite a number of empirical studies have been done to affirm this theory. In his book, Ariely (2008) describes an experiment where participants were asked to perform a mundane task on the computer — using the mouse to drag circles into squares. He found that people who were rewarded financially for participating exerted less effort than those who undertook the task as a favour (i.e. without being rewarded). Moreover, when rewards were given in the form of gifts (chocolates), the exchange stayed safely in the social world and the participants worked as hard as they did without reward out of *bona fide* goodwill.

In another study of day care centres in Israel, introducing a small fine on parents who turned up late to pick up their children resulted in more late pick-ups (Gneezy and Rustichini 2000). This was because introducing the financial penalty replaced social norms of guilt (for being late) with market norms of entitlement. The fine was seen as the price of lateness, and it granted the parents the right to decide for themselves how much lateness to "purchase". More interestingly, when the fine was subsequently removed, parents continued with their guilt-free (and now also fine-free) tardiness, reflecting that once social norms are replaced with market norms, the switch might well become an enduring one.

The fact that we live in two distinct worlds has important implications for governments hoping to shape certain behaviours through the use of economic incentives. In particular, they should be very careful in treading the delicate line between social and market norms. They should also understand the risk that there may be long-lasting damage to valuable social norms if they make use of economic incentives where inappropriate. An immediate example that comes to mind is that of organ trading. As Alvin Roth puts it, "Many people clearly regard monetary compensation for organ donation as something that transforms a good deed into a bad one" (Roth 2007, p. 45).

One of the considerations in the debate on whether to lift the ban on organ trading in Singapore was how social norms might change as a result. On one hand, the ban ought to be lifted because it prevented mutually beneficial exchanges from being realised. Without a market pricing mechanism, the supply of organs simply could not meet demand. On the other hand, allowing the sale of organs might reduce the willingness of people to donate, if as a result, altruistic acts were "transformed" into commercial transactions. The crowding out effect would be dramatically amplified if the sale of organs is widely considered to be repugnant. The government was careful to strike the right tone, steering away from any mention of "payment", which implies a commercial transaction. "Reimbursement" to "defray the costs or expenses" incurred by organ donors was the language that was eventually adopted in the Act.

The unintended effects of money may not always be as immediately obvious, and policymakers may not always exercise enough caution in using economic incentives to achieve policy outcomes. Consider, for example, the issue of fertility that has been a preoccupation of the Singapore government in the past two decades or so. To encourage more babies, the Children Development Co-Savings Scheme (more commonly known as the "Baby Bonus") provides cash handouts to help offset the costs of having children. However, for someone who is deciding whether or not to have children, knowing that she "will get a cash gift of up to S$4,000 each for [her] 1st and 2nd child and S$6,000 each for [her] 3rd and 4th child" (MCYS 2010, p. 1 of 2) is unlikely to induce her to have (more) children. While financial penalties may work in bringing down fertility rates (Singapore's experience in this respect in the 1960s and 1970s was extremely successful) because of people's loss aversion, it is unlikely that the reverse — of using financial rewards to raise fertility rates — would be similarly effective.

All this is not to say that financial inducements do not matter in influencing fertility rates. After all, the countries that have succeeded in reversing declining fertility rates — such as some of the northern European countries — all provide a wide range of financial support for parents, ranging from generous childcare support to paid maternity and paternity leave. But the manner in which the financial support is provided and the way it is framed probably matter more than the fact that it is provided. In these countries, the language used is *not* one of incentives and cash gifts, but that of social support. Neither do their societies view the comprehensive child-related benefits as monetary incentives to boost their fertility rates. Rather, the benefits are part of a wider social support system that includes unemployment insurance, disability benefits, heavily subsidised healthcare and publicly-financed pensions — all of which are an expression of these societies' egalitarian ethos, and all of which contribute to their sense of solidarity and cohesion. Norms of gender equity are also an important factor in explaining the Nordic countries' relatively high fertility rates. Paternity leave is a signal that fathers have an equal responsibility in raising children. It is this wider social compact that may explain their relatively high fertility rates, more so than any of their specific pro-natal "incentives".

Policymakers who hope to raise fertility rates ought to think about how government's financial support can crowd in people's motivation to have children and shift social attitudes and norms in the desired direction. Such shifts are more likely to occur through efforts to increase gender equity, more employers embracing family and child-friendly practices, and government framing the financial help it provides in the language of social support rather than incentives.

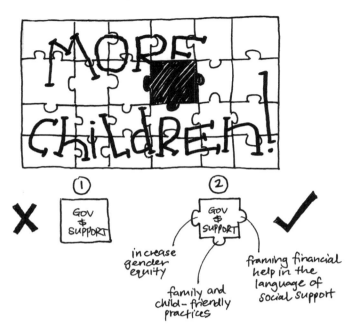

Policymakers who hope to raise fertility rates ought to think about how governments' financial support can crowd in people's motivation to have children and shift social attitudes and norms in the desired direction.

Getting Incentives and Norms Right

More broadly, policymakers need to consider the three-way relationship between regulations, incentives and norms. Economists have always argued against the use of arbitrary bans, prohibitions and regulatory diktats that prevent mutually beneficial trades between self-interested agents. Where there are costs involved that the transacting parties fail to account for (i.e. there are negative externalities present), the economist's prescription is not to ban these transactions altogether but to tax them to force the producer of the externality to take into account the costs he imposes on society. Pricing the externality is not only more efficient, but it also preserves choice for people to engage in those transactions if they are mutually advantageous for the transacting parties.

This approach of dealing with externalities has been widely used in Singapore. Examples include alcohol and tobacco duties (among the highest in the world), congestion charging, high taxes on vehicle ownership, and foreign worker levies on employers. However, many emerging policy problems that Singapore is likely to face in the medium to long term — inequality and sustainable development to cite just two — are complex ones that probably cannot be simply tackled by a simple application of taxes and subsidies. Effective policies will also need to shape social norms in the right directions — a point that cannot be over-emphasised.

Take inequality for instance. The conventional economic response to inequality is to increase taxes on the rich and increase social transfers (or lump sum transfers) to the poor. While these measures are necessary in an era of rising income inequality, the government should also think about how it can strengthen norms of inclusion and fairness. The recent introduction of the Workfare Income Supplement (WIS) in Singapore — a wage supplement for low-wage workers — is a case in point. As a negative income tax, it aims to "make work pay" and provides a stronger incentive for low-wage workers to stay employed. But more than that, it also supports norms of inclusion and fairness. A job is not just an income-generating activity; it also enables people to participate more fully in society. Meanwhile, taxpayers are more likely to see transfer payments as fair — and are more likely to support them — if individuals have to work to receive the supplement.

Market fundamentalists often decry the extensive role of the state in areas such as education, health and housing. They argue that even if the state needs to subsidise the provision of such services, they should do so by "mimicking" markets. Thus, a purist economics approach would advocate the privatisation of schools, healthcare and social housing, and the provision of lump-sum transfers or vouchers to citizens to consume these services. These measures, the market fundamentalist argues, will increase consumer choice, foster competition among providers and enhance economic efficiency. However, to the extent that such institutions are not just about efficient provision of services, but also about strengthening norms of inclusion and community, privatisation may well be a poor solution because it fails to take into account the positive externalities associated with public provision. Privatisation may also create more differentiated and fragmented systems that lead to uneven access, undermine social inclusion, and reduce citizens' willingness to finance the provision of these goods through their taxes.

We may also consider environmental sustainability. The economist's standard prescription for promoting energy conservation would be to tax the use of fossil fuels, while (possibly) subsidising renewable energy and energy efficiency measures. While there is merit in such policy measures, they are far more effective if supported by the right social norms and attitudes towards energy conservation. In countries which have successfully decoupled energy use from economic growth, changing social norms are as important as the use of economic incentives such as energy and carbon taxes. In Denmark and Sweden — two highly energy-efficient economies — reconstruction in the post-war years when materials were scarce played an important role in forging a national consensus on energy conservation, recycling and reducing waste.

This combination of incentives and norms should lie at the heart of any effort to promote sustainable development. Incentives (in the form of taxes and subsidies) without the supporting social norms can be deeply unpopular. Witness the riots every time governments in Southeast Asia try to remove economically inefficient fuel subsidies. This is so even if the fuel subsidies are replaced by more targeted and efficient ways of helping the poor. Conversely, social norms without the supporting incentives may diminish or lose their hold on people over time.

The lesson for policymakers in all these is not that the use of economic incentives does not work. Indeed, behavioural economists also highlight instances where financial incentives may crowd in intrinsic motivations or reinforce social norms.[1] What matters just as much as the policy itself is the *context* in which the policy is implemented and how it is framed. How is the policy presented and communicated? Does the policy work with, and support, desirable social norms such as those of inclusion and fairness? Does it try to harness people's motivations to do the right thing?

Conclusion

The use of market-based instruments and price incentives by governments to achieve policy goals is a reflection of a sound, rational approach to governance. This reliance on price incentives needs to be accompanied with a greater understanding of social norms and how they may interact with markets. This perspective is critical as many of the policy problems that governments have to deal with require not only the right incentives, but also the "right" social norms and attitudes.

Finally, policymakers should be conscious that they never start on a blank slate. The economic incentives they introduce will inevitably interact with existing social norms. Social norms can work with or against incentives in achieving a government's policy objectives. Being sensitive to what those norms are — and how they may be altered by incentives — will increasingly be an essential part of sound policymaking.

---

[1] Frey (1994) found that external interventions "crowd in intrinsic motivations if they are perceived to be acknowledging". That is, intrinsic motivations may be strengthened by financial incentives if they are perceived as an acknowledgement or appreciation of the agent's intrinsic motivation.

References

Alm, James, Gary McClelland and William Schulze (1999). "Changing the Social Norm of Tax Compliance by Voting." *KYKLOS*, Vol. 52, No. 2, pp. 141–171.

Ariely, Dan (2008). *Predictably Irrational: The Hidden Forces That Shape Our Decisions*. HarperCollins.

Bauman, Yoram (2009). "Stand-up Economist", viewed 10 August 2010, http://www.standupeconomist.com/blog/humor/you-might-be-an-economist-if/

Frey, Bruno (1994). "How Intrinsic Motivation is Crowded Out and In."*Rationality and Society*, Vol. 6, No. 3, pp. 334–352.

Gneezy, Uri and Aldo Rustichini (2000). "A Fine is a Price." *Journal of Legal Studies*, Vol. 29, No. 1, pp. 1–17.

Lessig, Lawrence (1995). "The Regulation of Social Meaning." *The University of Chicago Law Review*, Vol. 62, No. 3, pp. 943–1045.

Ministry of Community, Youth and Sports, Singapore (2010). "Children Development Co-Savings (Baby Bonus) Scheme", viewed 10 August 2010, https://www.babybonus.gov.sg/bbss/html/index.html

Posner, Eric (2000). "Law and Social Norms: The Case of Tax Compliance." *Virginia Law Review*, Vol. 86, No. 8, pp. 1781–1819.

Roth, Alvin (2007). "Repugnance as a Constraint on Markets." *Journal of Economic Perspectives*, Vol. 21, No. 3, pp. 37–58.

Sunstein, Cass (1996). "Social Norms and Social Roles." *Columbia Law Review*, Vol. 96, No. 4, pp. 903–968.

Titmuss, Richard (1971). *The Gift Relationship: From Blood Donations to Social Policy*. Pantheon Books.

PART II

CHAPTER 3

A BEHAVIOURAL PERSPECTIVE TO MANAGING TRAFFIC CONGESTION IN SINGAPORE

LEONG Wai Yan and LEW Yii Der

"Driving in traffic, one is often hard-pressed to think of fellow travellers as rational. They swerve across multiple lanes to make a turn, race to get to the next red light, slow to ogle fender-benders and engage in other roadway antics. Yet for the most part transportation planners and policymakers treat drivers — as well as transit riders and other travellers — as basically rational."

Mark Solof (2010)

Introduction

As a small, highly urbanised city-state, Singapore has had to apply economic analysis more aggressively than most other jurisdictions in the search for traffic management solutions. Congestion charging and the use of high vehicle taxes to limit vehicle ownership are straight out of economics textbooks. Standard economic prescriptions, however, hinge on narrowly defined assumptions about the rationality of individuals and organisations. Empirical findings from behavioural economics have turned up often surprising and counter-intuitive results that call these assumptions into question, and these may also suggest novel approaches to policy design today.

This chapter will look at how key findings from behavioural economics provide valuable alternative perspectives into some of

Singapore's traffic demand management measures, such as the Area Licensing Scheme, the Vehicle Quota System and the Electronic Road Pricing system. A richer understanding of people's actual preferences and their responses to these policy measures can provide fresh guidance on the future design of land transport and congestion management policies.

Area Licensing Scheme (1975): Imposing Road Charges

The Area Licensing Scheme (ALS) was introduced in 1975 to manage traffic congestion in the city centre. The scheme required motorists to purchase a paper licence if they wished to enter a cordoned area known as the Restricted Zone (RZ) during the morning peak hours. When it was first implemented, the ALS licence cost S$3 for a day or S$60 for a month.

When the ALS was introduced, vehicle taxes and parking charges in the city centre were also raised. The bus network was also enhanced to give commuters more travel options. Taken together, these measures resulted in an immediate 76% cut in the number of cars entering the RZ during licensing hours (Behbehani *et al.* 1984). Concurrently, the proportion of bus trips increased from 33% to 46% of inbound RZ trips. Transport researchers generally agree that the ALS was a success.

The standard consumer theory in economics undoubtedly provides one explanation for the drop in cars bound for the RZ. By raising the price of a car trip while improving the substitutability of public transport alternatives, demand for car travel into the RZ can be reduced. However, recent findings by behavioural economists suggest that more may be going on than just the impact of price incentives.

A recent study by Shampanier *et al.* (2007) on the power of free may help us further understand the ALS' success. The study found that people strongly preferred free items, even when a better deal was available at a nominal cost. In one experiment, people were given a choice between expensive Lindt chocolate truffles for 15 cents and ordinary Hershey's Kisses for 1 cent.

	Choose Between		Choose Between	
	15c	1c	14c	Free
Lindt Truffles	73%	—	31%	—
Hershey's Kisses	—	27%	—	69%

Exhibit 1: Significant demand shift to a free item.

Sensing a good deal, 73% went for the truffles. With another group, they dropped the price of both the truffles and the Kisses by 1 cent apiece: 14 cents for the truffles and free for the Kisses. Under these conditions, the authors found a significant switch in taste: 69% chose the free Hershey Kisses instead (see Exhibit 1).

This strong preference for zero cost is a human psychological trait with no straightforward explanation from conventional economic theory. Standard cost-benefit analysis tells us that the net benefits of both products remain the same in both scenarios and hence there should be no change to the proportion of respondents choosing the truffles when the kisses were priced at zero. However, the results of the experiment showed that people saw zero as more than just another (low) price.

The power of free also suggests that once a free item is priced above zero, demand for that item could plummet significantly, more than what conventional economics would predict. Could this have happened in the case of the ALS? While it is difficult to attribute the 76% fall in car trips into the RZ to either standard or behavioural economic forces in the absence of a suitable control, what we now know about the zero-price effect gives us some hints that standard economics does not fully account for the strength of motorists' aversion to the ALS.

If people are reacting to the non-zero characteristic of the price, rather than to the price level per se, then as long as a previously free item is priced, a significant cutback in demand would ensue, at a magnitude somewhat independent of the price change. In the road pricing context, this would imply that a S$1 charge on a previously uncharged road would impact traffic volumes by an order of magnitude similar to a S$3 charge. Recent evidence seems to bear this theory out. In April 2008, when a S$1 road pricing charge was introduced to arterial roads like Toa Payoh Lorong 6 and Upper Boon Keng Road, traffic volumes fell by a sizeable 30% to 57%. The upper end of this range is not a lot lower compared to the reduction in traffic flows brought about by the initial implementation of the ALS, considering that S$3 in 1975 meant a lot more in real terms than S$1 today.

Conversely, the power of free also implies that beyond the initial imposition of a price, further increases in price of the same magnitude can be expected to be less effective. For instance, imposing a S$1 charge on a previously uncharged road would achieve a significant reduction in road usage, but increasing it from S$1 to S$2 would produce a much smaller reduction.

Car pools provide another interesting perspective on the power of free. As cars with a minimum of 4 persons were initially exempted from ALS charges, there was a 17 percentage point increase in the car pool market share, out of the total number of cars entering the RZ (Behbehani *et al.* 1984). Subsequently, the ALS exemption policy resulted in an unusual phenomenon. Drivers would pick up strangers at special car pool pick-up points in order to enter the city without paying. Likewise, car pool passengers were willing to share car space with other strangers to get a free ride into the city. In the Singapore context where there is a strong aversion to sharing vehicles with strangers, the power of free car pools appeared strong enough to convince a good number of people to overcome their reservations about car sharing.[1]

In fact, the popularity of free car pools grew significantly and became so attractive that bus patronage was negatively affected. The government eventually decided to abolish the ALS exemption

---

[1] As an example of how strangers are generally reluctant to share space in the same car, a scheme to encourage taxi sharing among taxi users heading in the same direction did not enjoy a high take-up rate and was eventually discontinued.

for car pools in 1989, and by doing so, the era of car pools — Singapore-style — came to an end.

The policy conclusion for transport authorities is that the elimination of free roads has a definite impact on drivers' behaviour. People are so attached to "free" that when roads are priced to manage congestion, travel patterns undergo significant shifts to mitigate the feeling of loss. Unfortunately, the corollary to the power of free is the difficult task of convincing car users to give up free use of the roads in the first place. The numerous abortive attempts around the world to introduce congestion charging underscore this point.

Vehicle Quota System (1990): Fairness in Auctions

For many years, the government tried to curtail vehicle population growth by introducing, then progressively raising, the Additional Registration Fee. An *ad valorem* tax, the fee went as high as 175% of the market value of the vehicle. Consistent with the principles of standard economics, the government hoped that high vehicle taxes would moderate the increase in the car population, but this proved inadequate. A new policy tool was needed that would more directly control the vehicle population.

In 1990, Singapore introduced a Vehicle Quota System. Under this system, anyone who wishes to buy a new car must first obtain a Certificate of Entitlement (COE). The number of COEs available each year is determined by the allowable annual vehicle growth rate. This was fixed at 3% from 1990 and reduced to 1.5% from May 2009.

With a limited supply of COEs, standard economics would prescribe an auction mechanism to allocate the COEs efficiently. But it appears that the general population is not just concerned about economic efficiency alone. Indeed, people dislike the idea of auctions as Kahneman *et al.* (1986) discovered when they polled 191 adult residents of Vancouver for their response to the following situation:

> Due to the popularity of a football team, there is now a shortage of tickets to the next match. The organisers can elect to sell tickets in the following ways. (1) By auction: The tickets are

sold to the highest bidders. (2) By lottery: The tickets are sold to the people whose names are drawn. (3) By queue: The tickets are sold on a first-come-first-served basis.

Allocation Method	Most Fair (%)	Least Fair (%)
Auction	4	75
Lottery	28	18
Queue	68	7

Exhibit 2:   Ranking of allocation methods.

When asked to rank the three allocation methods in terms of fairness, a large majority of the respondents thought that the queue was the fairest way and the auction the least fair, as shown in Exhibit 2. This preference is opposite to a ranking by an economic efficiency criterion, which would put the auction above the lottery and above the queue.

Kahneman *et al.* concluded that the findings seem to be driven by some general rules of fairness that are held in common by a community. One of these rules states that it is unfair for someone to exploit an increase in market power at the direct expense of someone else.

This rule of fairness appears to transcend culture and is apparent in the Singapore context as well. During the early stages of the COE debate when the feasibility of using an auction to allocate the COEs was discussed, the Singapore public raised concerns that those who could afford bigger luxury cars would use their superior "market power" to outbid small car buyers.

What was the policy response to these concerns? Firstly, conventional economics still prevailed. A competitive bidding system was still adopted, with all successful bidders paying the lowest successful bid price.[2] Nevertheless, to address the social equity

---

[2] When the COE open bidding system was introduced in 2002, some changes were made to the auction process and successful bidders pay the highest unsuccessful bid price + S$1.

concerns, a decision was taken to classify vehicles into different categories, as follows:

- Category 1: Small cars (engine capacity of 1,000 cc and below)
- Category 2: Medium-sized cars (engine capacity of 1,001 cc to 1,600 cc)
- Category 3: Big cars (engine capacity of 1,601 cc to 2,000 cc);
- Category 4: Luxury cars (engine capacity of 2,001 cc and above)
- Category 5: Goods vehicles and buses
- Category 6: Motorcycles
- Category 7: "Open" (for any kind of vehicles)

Each category had its own COE quota and COEs obtained under one category could only be used to buy a vehicle from that category.[3]

The quota system illustrates a more general principle about policymaking in Singapore. While the conventional economic prescription may guide the overall policy direction, behavioural considerations help to tailor a solution that better meets the concerns and aspirations of the population. Hence, although having a single COE category is economically more efficient, separate categories were introduced to improve public acceptance of the scheme and to address concerns of social equity.[4]

Electronic Road Pricing System (1998): From Sunk Costs to Variable Charges

In 1998, the ALS gave way to the Electronic Road Pricing (ERP) system. This was an important shift in Singapore's road pricing

---

[3] The exception is the "Open" category whose COE can be used to purchase any type of vehicle. This is meant to give the VQS greater flexibility to respond to changing demand for different types of vehicles.

[4] Categorisation is not economically efficient as it may lead to situations where the quota is very binding in some categories and not binding in others (Tan 2001). This is one reason for the Vehicle Quota System Review Committee's recommendedation in 1999 to consolidate the four car categories into two, quoting examples of economic inefficiencies associated with too many quota categories (Land Transport Authority of Singapore 1999).

strategy. The manual ALS system charged motorists a fixed fee for the day or the month, regardless of actual usage. The ERP, on the other hand, provides greater flexibility to set congestion charges based on prevailing traffic conditions, which vary with location and time of the day. It is also based on a pay-as-you-use principle, where the congestion charge is instantly deducted from a stored-value card in an In-Vehicle Unit every time the vehicle uses a priced road (Chin and Menon 2004).

What we know of people's behaviour suggests that charging a fixed fee — as in the case of the ALS — may lead to more, rather than less, consumption. This is termed the sunk cost effect — the tendency to continue in an activity once an investment of time, money or energy has been made. Standard economics states that sunk costs are irrelevant to current decisions — which should only be based on a consideration of current costs and benefits — and should therefore not be taken into account. However, it appears that people routinely do the opposite.

In one experiment designed by Arkes and Blumer (1985), people buying season tickets to a theatre group's performance were randomly given one of three different classes of tickets: full price tickets at $15, tickets with a small $2 discount and tickets with a sizeable $7 discount. If these people behaved like homo economicus (rational man) and weighed the marginal costs and benefits of attending each play, then the average number of plays attended should not differ across the three groups as the discounts were randomly assigned. However, what Arkes and Blumer found was that those who paid full price, i.e. a higher sunk cost, attended significantly more plays than the other groups, at least in the first half of the season (see Exhibit 3).

Viewed from this perspective, designing the ERP on a pay-per-use principle is thus a better option, compared to fixed fee charging like the ALS. As the Arkes and Blumer experiment shows, the latter option might encourage even more consumption of limited road space.

Similarly, because sunk costs matter, the high fixed cost of car ownership can be inimical to the policy objective of restraining

Types of Tickets	Average Number of Plays Attended
Full Price ($15)	4.11
$2 discount	3.32
$7 discount	3.29

Exhibit 3: People who paid higher sunk costs attended more plays.

Source: Arkes and Blumer (1985).

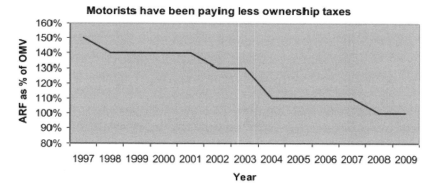

Exhibit 4: Changes to additional registration fee for cars from 1997 to 2009.

Source: Land Transport Authority of Singapore.

car usage. Thus, instead of simply relying on high car ownership cost to manage congestion on the road, the government has, over the years, reduced vehicle taxes and shifted towards usage charges (through the ERP) to manage the demand for road space. Exhibit 4 traces changes to the Additional Registration Fee[5] for cars. It illustrates the government's move to rely less on fixed ownership cost to manage congestion with the introduction of ERP.

---

[5] The Additional Registration Fee (ARF) was introduced in 1972 as a fiscal deterrent to curb the growth in car population. It is pegged at a certain percentage of the car's assessed value, i.e. its Open Market Value (OMV).

In Singapore, owning a car will always be a substantial outlay. There is a limit to how much the government can reduce the fixed upfront cost of owning a car, given that COE prices are market determined. Once they buy a car, car owners will have an inherent tendency to maximise its usage, especially if COE prices are high. ERP then becomes an even more critical policy tool to mitigate the sunk cost effect in an environment of high ownership costs. The ever-present challenge for transport policy is striking the appropriate balance between using ownership control and implementing usage charges to manage overall road congestion.

Refining the ERP System: Making Charges More Salient

Behavioural economists have observed that people use cognitive processes known as mental accounting to record their financial transactions and assign activities to specific accounts (Thaler 1999). In particular, if payment is decoupled from consumption, i.e. put in separate mental accounts, the perceived cost of consumption is reduced and this encourages more consumption, which is what happens when purchases are made on credit. Conversely, the experience of "having the meter running" is generally unpleasant to most people as it is both salient and directly linked to the consumption activity. For example, Thaler noted that many car owners would be financially better off selling their cars and taking taxis to the supermarket. But this is rarely done because paying $10 for each taxi trip seems to raise the cost of groceries in ways that paying off a monthly car loan do not.

With this insight, one way to enhance the effectiveness of ERP is to make ERP charges more salient, i.e. make people take greater account of the charges. To this end, the Land Transport Authority of Singapore has installed real-time electronic display of ERP charges at all gantries since 2008 (Exhibit 5). This is expected to raise motorists' awareness of the actual cost of a trip and help them

Exhibit 5: ERP gantry with real-time display of ERP charges.
Source: Land Transport Authority of Singapore.

make a considered decision, for example, whether to shift some trips to a less congested time period where the ERP charges are lower or zero.

The next generation of In-Vehicle Units will also help to make ERP charges more salient to the motorist. Unlike the current units which only display the balance in the stored-value card, the new ones will display the actual charge incurred each time the vehicle passes under an ERP gantry.

Effecting Shifts to Public Transport: Making Savings More Salient

Traditional economic theory assumes that someone makes a choice, for instance, deciding to drive to work, after having fully considered all relevant costs, such as daily parking fees, petrol costs, ERP and other vehicle operating costs. However, mental accounting "blocks" these costs from being amalgamated, i.e. money is not fungible. Recent evidence from LTA's stated preference studies show that motorists are about 3 times more sensitive to a S$1 increase in ERP compared to a S$1 increase in fuel costs, for the same journey. From a rational economic perspective, it should not matter whether the increase in cost arises because of ERP or petrol; but from a behavioural perspective, petrol prices or petrol tax needs to increase by S$3 to effect the same change as a S$1 increase in ERP. This phenomenon arises possibly because compared to ERP, parking and petrol costs are less salient as these latter accounts are accessed on a weekly or monthly basis, not daily. Therefore, the total cost of daily driving appears lower than it really is,[6] suggesting that any potential savings from switching from cars to public transport would be underestimated in the minds of car owners.

To overcome the mental accounting problem, a number of creative and intriguing possibilities exist. For example, Adelaide has developed a web-based Personal Savings Calculator, with the aim of making the savings from switching to public transport more salient (see Exhibit 6). In the imaginary world of rational agents, such a calculator would be unnecessary, but it appears that people need vivid reminders to make better decisions for themselves.

The calculator estimates the total potential savings from taking public transport, taken across all categories of driving costs. For car drivers who are concerned about reducing their carbon footprints, the Personal Savings Calculator also provides estimated savings of greenhouse gases. More importantly, the monetary savings are framed not just on a weekly basis, but aggregated into an annual amount, which is then mapped to a tangible consumption good, such as a beach holiday. This point of reference helps car users to see what they can gain by switching to public transport.

---

[6] In many instances, the monthly parking cost is deducted automatically from the payroll, making it even less salient to the motorist.

Q. How did they afford this holiday?

A. They caught the Adelaide Metro
...and saved over $11,000* a year!

The Adelaide Metro Personal Savings Calculator	
How many kilometres from work do you live?	25 (5kms minimum)
How many times per week do you travel to work?	5
How many weeks per year do you work? (full-time employment with 4-weeks annual leave is 46.2 weeks a year)	49
Choose vehicle 1 - the vehicle you drive to work in (examples of vehicle types are provided here) Your petrol consumption is determined by your choice of vehicle. The cost of petrol is the average price of unleaded fuel in Adelaide from May 2009 (118.1cpl).	Large Car ▼
Choose your daily price paid for parking (city 'Early Bird' average is $11.00 per day)	$ 11.00 per day
Choose your ticket type New fares displayed effective 5 July 2009 (Multitrip represents the best value, offering customers 10 trips for less than the price of 7) (examples of ticket types are provided here)	Single-Trip $4.40 ▼
Click for your Savings	Calculate
YOUR TOTAL Weekly Saving for vehicle 1 is	$76.90
YOUR TOTAL Annual Saving for vehicle 1 is	$3768.10

Weekly greenhouse gas emissions (kgs)	63.00
Annual greenhouse gas emissions (kgs)	308.70

Exhibit 6: Public transport savings calculator in Adelaide.
Source: Adelaide Metro (2010).

Conclusion

Behavioural economists have made much progress in recent years in understanding the psychological basis for our human preferences and tendencies. Unlike standard economic theories which have an established history of influence in policy debates, behavioural findings are only just beginning to make inroads into the public policy discussion. As these become more widely understood and accepted, behavioural economics has the potential to help governments design more effective and innovative policies.

Singapore's experience in managing road congestion offers some interesting examples of how concepts from behavioural economics can be applied to manage vehicle ownership and road usage. Behavioural economics also provides some clues as to why individuals feel unhappier over an increase in the congestion charge than an increase in petrol costs of the same magnitude. Finally, it suggests ways in which transport policymakers can induce a switch to public transport by making the savings from using public transport more salient.

References

Adelaide Metro (2010). "Public Transport Savings Calculator in Adelaide", viewed 20 December 2010, http://www.adelaidemetro.com.au/general/save_10000.html.

Arkes, Hal and Catherine Blumer (1985). "The Psychology of Sunk Cost." *Organizational Behavior and Human Decision Processes*, Vol. 35, No. 1, pp. 124–140.

Behbehani, R., V. Setty Pendakur and Alan Armstrong-Wright (1984). "Singapore Area Licensing Scheme: A Review of the Impact." Water Supply and Development Department Mimeo, World Bank, Washington D.C., July, pp. 49–50.

Chin, Anthony and A. P. G. Menon (2004). "ERP in Singapore — What's been Learnt from 5 Years of Operation?" *Traffic Engineering & Control*, February 2004.

Kahneman, Daniel, Jack Knetsch and Richard Thaler (1986). "Fairness and the Assumptions of Economics." *Journal of Business*, Vol. 59, No. 4, S285–S300.

Land Transport Authority of Singapore (1999), "Report of the Vehicle Quota System Review Committee, March 1999", viewed 20 December 2010, http://www.lta.gov.sg/corp_info/doc/VQS%20Review%201999.pdf

Shampanier, Kristina, Nina Mazar and Dan Ariely (2007). "Zero as a Special Price: The True Value of Free Products." *Marketing Science*, Vol. 26, No. 6, pp. 742–757.

Solof, Mark (2010). "Travellers Behaving Badly: Behavioural Economics Offers Insights and Strategies for Improving Transportation." *InTransition Magazine*, Spring/Summer 2010 Issue, viewed 20 December 2010, http://www.intransitionmag.org/spring-summer_2010/behavioral_economics_and_transportation.aspx

Tan, Ling Hui (2001). "Rationing Rules and Outcomes: The Experience of Singapore's Vehicle Quota System." *International Monetary Fund Working Paper*, WP/01/136.

Thaler, Richard (1999). "Mental Accounting Matters." *Journal of Behavioral Decision Making*, Vol. 12, No. 3, pp. 183–206.

CHAPTER 4

CAN PSYCHOLOGY SAVE THE PLANET AND IMPROVE OUR ENVIRONMENT?

Philip ONG

"... we're living in a finite world, one in which resource constraints are becoming increasingly binding... It will require that we gradually change the way we live, adapting our economy and our lifestyles to the reality of more expensive resources."

Paul Krugman (2010)

Introduction

Would you be tempted to buy a Toyota Prius if your neighbour drove one? Would you recycle your plastic bottles if everyone in your block knew whether or not you did? Would you refrain from littering if you saw a sign telling you not to? Will paying ten-cents for a plastic carrier motivate you to bring your own bag? Will a ten-cent rebate for not using the supermarket's plastic bags make you do the same?

A growing body of evidence suggests that people can be motivated to behave in more environmentally friendly ways by appealing to their need for belonging and a positive self-image, their preference for immediate gratification, their aversion to losses, and their reliance on simple rules of thumb.

This chapter first reviews how a conventional economist would deal with environmental externalities such as pollution or the carbon emissions that cause climate change. It argues that the principal approach recommended by textbook economics — of using externality charges to force the producers or end-consumers of these externalities to "internalise" the social costs of their actions — is necessary but not always sufficient. The chapter then examines how environmental policies can be augmented and improved by an understanding of the human traits and heuristics of image motivation, loss aversion, saliency, mental accounting and discounting. Finally, it explores the relationship between our pursuit of status and the quest for environmental sustainability.

The Standard Economics Approach to the Environment

The standard economics approach to environmental problems starts with an analysis of how incentives of producers are not properly aligned with those of society. The owner of a factory that causes pollution is presumed to take into account only the private costs of his actions. He does not consider the social costs — or the harm imposed on the rest of society — of his production activities. Left to itself, the factory will produce more than what is socially desirable because the costs of pollution are not borne by the factory owner, but by the rest of society. The factory owner cares only about his own profits and so has little incentive to cut down on his level of activity or to implement technologies that would allow him to produce the same amount of output with less pollution. This misalignment of incentives between the producer and the rest of society is at the heart of all externalities. Negative externalities arise whenever there is a divergence between private and social costs — and the latter exceeds the former.

The existence of externalities is an important exception to one of the general rules of conventional economics — that unregulated, competitive markets produce efficient, socially desirable outcomes. Where there are externalities involved, the free market outcome is either one of over-production (in the case of negative externalities such as pollution) or under-production (in the case of positive externalities such as those arising from basic research or public health).

The same analysis extends to the problem of global warming. The carbon emissions that each country produces contribute to the total amount of carbon in the atmosphere and hence to climate change. Climate change is the quintessential "tragedy of the commons". A single country that drastically reduces its carbon emissions is unable to solve the problem because another might decide to increase its carbon emissions, leaving the total level unchanged. In the absence of a binding agreement for all (or most) countries to reduce their carbon emissions, it is rational for individual countries to ignore the global consequences of their carbon emissions by pursuing self-interested goals. More effective mitigation of climate change requires the incentives of individual countries to be properly aligned with those of the global society.

The standard economics solution to the problem of environmental externalities, such as pollution and climate change, is to establish a price for these externalities. This can be achieved either through a tax on the externality — a carbon tax for instance — or a cap-and-trade system in which the government sets a quota for the total amount of externalities that can be produced and allows for the "pollution permits" to be traded. A tax prices the externality directly and forces the producer to take into account the costs of his actions on society. This creates incentives for him to cut down on his production of the externality. If the government can quantify the social cost of an externality, the sensible course of action would be to tax it. With a tax on the externality, its price is known upfront although the quantity of the externality that is eventually produced remains uncertain.

A cap-and-trade system also limits the production of the externality. By creating a market for the externality, a cap-and-trade system allows for market participants to "discover" the price of the externality. Again, this price has the desired effect of creating incentives for producers to reduce their production of the externality. Where the government is less sure about the social cost of the externality but has information about the quantity of the externality it wants to control, a cap-and-trade system makes sense. With a cap-and-trade system, the quantity is known but the price of the permits that are traded is not known *ex ante* and is subject to discovery by the market participants. The closest example of such a system in Singapore is the vehicle quota system in which the government sets the number of vehicle ownership permits (known as Certificates of Entitlement) that are released annually, while a twice-monthly auction process determines the price of these permits. Such a system results in quantity certainty but not price certainty.

Both taxation and a cap-and-trade system share the standard economics emphasis: that of getting incentives right. This differs from a regulatory approach that focuses on setting minimum mandatory standards. In dealing with environmental externalities, governments have tended to rely more on such regulations than on environmental taxes. For instance, governments often set regulatory standards on the amount of pollutants (for example, sulphur dioxide) that a factory or power plant may emit. There are sometimes good reasons for imposing these "green" standards. Environmental and technical standards for equipment help to create a level playing field among producers when there are high costs involved in switching to cleaner technologies. Standards overcome coordination problems and realise network effects and economies of scale more quickly. Regulation can be the more cost-effective policy instrument when there are large numbers of people individually generating small negative externalities (for instance, through energy use) that can be large in aggregate. When consumers are not sensitive to prices, it may also make sense to rely on regulations rather than incentives.

Nonetheless, in most cases, economists favour the use of incentives over the use of regulations or minimum standards. Taxes or a cap-and-trade system produce continuous incentives for producers to reduce their pollution levels. Environmental regulations that stipulate minimum standards provide no financial incentive for a producer to surpass those standards. Pricing the externality on the other hand means that every reduction in pollution levels translates into cost savings for the producer.

Approaches based on economic incentives and minimum standards are not the only options open to environmental policymakers. Neither are they always sufficient on their own. The lack of information or feedback to users may limit the effectiveness of economic incentives. For instance, taxes on energy use may not be as effective as they could be if people are not conscious of how much they can save by cutting down on consumption or by switching to more energy-efficient appliances. Programmes that encourage recycling by giving rebates to people for not using plastic bags may flounder if people deem these rebates too small to be worth their effort. Energy-efficient appliances — which may cost more upfront but are actually cheaper over the product's life cycle — may not be widely adopted if people are not able to make these calculations or if they are put off by the higher upfront costs they have to pay.

A third approach, the one favoured by behavioural economists, is to develop a deeper understanding of what drives us into adopting environmentally sustainable practices, and to use that understanding to improve environmental policies. This approach holds the promise of informing policymakers how to intelligently combine the use of minimum standards, incentives and feedback to consumers.

The Psychology of Environmentally Sustainable Behaviour

There are several concepts we can borrow from behavioural economics to explain the psychology of environmentally friendly behaviours.

Image Motivation

The first is the effect of image motivation. A lot of what we do is driven by our social relationships and our desire for social acceptance. We are often preoccupied with what people say about us, what they might be thinking, whether they are kind or rude to us, and how we should respond.

What does this have to do with getting people to make more environmentally friendly choices? Quite a bit, as it turns out.

A study found that the purchase of a hybrid vehicle is not motivated by fuel-saving concerns (Heffner *et al.* 2005). Lengthy interviews with Northern Californian hybrid owners suggested that the real impetus is one's own image as a responsible green citizen of the world. The symbolic effects of owning a hybrid vehicle are at least as powerful as, if not more so than, the functional benefits of saving energy. The idea that cars play a role in identity formation is not new — it is, in fact, the basis for many car commercials. Cars are used to establish a positive self-image and to communicate that image to other people.

Effective environmental programmes often leverage this very human concern about what other people think of us. An example is the United Kingdom's Zero Waste Place initiative (Local Government Association 2009), under which neighbourhoods that have achieved notable environment improvements are accredited by the government under the spotlight of local and national media. Such improvements involved going beyond the national target to recycle and compost at least 40% of household waste by 2010. Successful applications received funding for expansion and development of measures to help attain the waste target. While the initial take-up of the scheme was low, press attention associated with the project raised the awareness of residents and increased participation rates. Some residents were also inspired by the work on their street and began modifying their own homes to be more energy efficient.

Arguably, the introduction of the Mandatory Energy Labelling for household air-conditioners and refrigerators in Singapore has resulted in an increase in the sales of three- to four-tick[1] appliances not just because rational households think they will save money, but also because for the environmentally conscious, purchasing an energy-efficient appliance burnishes their own self-image as good stewards of the environment.

We will return to the relationship between social status, self image and the environment at the end of this chapter.

Loss Aversion

In 1979, Kahneman and Tversky presented an idea called prospect theory, which contended that people value gains and losses differently (Kahneman and Tversky 1979). According to prospect theory, losses have more emotional impact than equivalent gains. For example, if you were a rational individual, the amount of utility

---

[1] Appliances are rated on a scale of one to four ticks with four ticks being the most energy efficient.

gained from receiving $50 should be equal to a situation in which you gained $100 and then lost $50. In both situations, the end result is a net gain of $50. However, despite the fact that you still end up with a $50 gain in both cases, most people view a single gain of $50 more favourably than gaining $100 and then losing $50. As behavioural economists have found, people often care more about avoiding losses than pursuing gains of the same size.

This has implications for how we structure incentives to encourage environmentally-friendly behaviours such as recycling. It suggests that charging people who do not recycle is more effective than rewarding people who do. Charging 10 cents for a plastic bag would be more effective than giving a 10-cent rebate for not using one. For example, customers in Hong Kong are charged HK$0.50 (about S$0.10) for a plastic bag at major retailers. A year after its implementation, a dramatic reduction of 90% in the use of plastic bags was reported. Charging for a plastic bag is however still not widely practised by retailers in Singapore and many other countries. In the absence of similar legislation and left to their own devices, most retailers have simply turned to the more palatable option of rebates and campaigns, with predictably limited success.

Deposit refund schemes to encourage recycling are also more effective than schemes which pay people to recycle. This is because consumers loathe losing the deposit they pay on plastic and glass bottles if they do not recycle them. Under a deposit refund scheme consumers pay an upfront deposit every time they purchase beverages in plastic bottles or metal cans. They can get back their deposits only by returning their bottles and cans to recycling machines or to grocery stores. Behavioural economics tells us that such a system of deposit refund works better because it takes advantage of people's loss aversion, which is stronger than their desire to pursue gains. Longstanding deposit refund schemes in Denmark and Sweden for beverage containers (glass, metal, plastic) illustrate this, with a high returns percentage of more than 80%.

The establishment of deposit refund schemes clearly requires some form of government legislation and facilitation. It is unlikely that industry, left to its own devices, is able to develop a nation-wide scheme in which every bottle or can is marked and every grocery store or supermarket is required to accept recycled bottles or cans.

Of course, consumers would prefer a plain vanilla incentive scheme to one where they are clearly paying for their own incentives. Such a preference is rooted precisely in the loss aversion that a deposit refund scheme exploits to shape behaviour. This poses a challenge to obtaining public buy-in to such a scheme. Consumers first have to be convinced of the need for recycling and understand that incentives have to be paid for, and it is the consumer who invariably pays, whether directly or indirectly (through higher prices). The advantage of a deposit refund scheme is that this is done transparently and in a way that alters behaviour more effectively.

Another dimension of loss aversion that environmental policymakers should pay attention to is the difference between willingness to pay and willingness to accept. Standard economics assumes that the price which we are willing to pay for an item that we do not own is the same as the price at which we will accept for a similar item that we own. So in cost-benefit analysis for instance, it should not matter whether people are asked what they would pay for a proposed improvement (say a proposed bridge or a new subway line) or what they would want to be paid if the proposed improvement did not materialise.

Loss aversion however means that people typically set much higher prices to give up something than what they are prepared to pay to obtain it. For instance, a person's asking price for a mug he already owns tends to be higher than the price he would be willing to pay for the same mug (if he did not already own it). So what "price" should environmental policymakers use — the price that people are willing to pay (say to avoid pollution) or the price that they would accept (to put up with the pollution)? Generally, if people are asked to accept a loss or a decline relative to the status quo, policymakers should use the willingness-to-accept measure. If an improvement to the status quo is proposed, the willingness-to-pay measure should be used. Since environmental issues (such as pollution) often involve losses relative to the status quo, it appears that environmental policymakers should rely mostly on willingness-to-accept measures in determining the costs or benefits of their policy interventions.

Saliency or Availability Bias

People tend to heavily weigh their decisions towards more recent, more vivid and more widely known information, making any new opinion biased toward whatever information that can be easily recalled. Suppose you see a car accident along a stretch of road that you regularly drive on to get to work. Chances are that you will drive more cautiously for the next week or so. Although the road might be no more dangerous than before, seeing the accident causes you to overreact, but you will be back to your old driving habits by the following week when that information of the accident is no longer salient.

Cheap and simple measures that make an issue more salient and visible can be highly effective. Examples in Singapore include prominent signs displaying fines for littering, and stickers reminding users to turn off the lights. Some companies have also included a default message at the end of all emails to remind readers to think twice before printing the email.

Similarly, our energy consumption patterns may also be shaped by whether and how we receive feedback on our use of electricity. Smart meters — which measure a household's use of energy in real time — may be more effective in encouraging us to cut down on electricity use than the feedback we obtain through monthly utility bills. In Singapore, utility bills allow households to compare their energy use across recent months and against the national average. Such information is certainly useful. But monthly bills do not tell a household which appliances use more electricity than others. Neither are they able to tell us in real time the amount of electricity we are consuming — and more importantly, how much we are paying for it. Home energy display monitors and Home Energy Management Systems (HEMS) — which have started to be available in the market — provide this information in a timely and salient way, increasing the likelihood that households will act on that information.

Mental Accounting

People tend to allocate their money to separate accounts based on a variety of subjective criteria, such as the source of the money and the intent for each account. For example, some people may have a special "money jar" set aside for a vacation or a new home, while still carrying substantial credit card debt. In this case, rather than saving for a new home, the most logical course of action would be to use the funds in the jar to pay off the expensive debt. This seems simple enough, but people often do not behave this way. This is because of the personal value that people place on particular assets. For instance, people may feel that money saved for a new home or their children's college fund is too "important" to relinquish. As a result, this "important" account may not be touched at all, even if it is sensible to do so in the overall scheme of financial management.

Another aspect of mental accounting is that people treat money differently depending on its source. Logically, where the money came from should not determine how much of it one spends. Yet people tend to spend a lot more of their "found" money, such as work bonuses and gifts, compared to a similar amount of money that is normally expected, such as from their pay checks or even from rebates (which suggest a return to the status quo).

Why is this relevant to environmental policies? Suppose the government introduced new environmental levies or taxes. Should it set aside and earmark these revenues for specific environmental purposes? Standard economics says this practice of earmarking (or hypothecation) is sub-optimal: all government revenues, regardless of their origins, are fungible and should be put to their best public use. But if people have different mental accounts, the earmarking of revenues from environmental levies and taxes may actually make their imposition more acceptable to the public.

Charging a waste levy to discourage excessive waste disposal would be more acceptable to the general public if the revenue was earmarked for programmes to help households recycle more of their waste. Another example would be to channel revenue from an electricity conservation tax to programmes that will help households save energy. This is already practised in places like the state of California, where residents pay a Public Goods Charge (a small charge per kWh paid by end users), which is then used to finance rebates which reduce the price of energy-efficient lighting and appliances, as well as other energy efficiency programmes.

Discounting

Government interventions to promote energy efficiency have often been held hostage to a tacit assumption that if saving a lot more energy were possible at an affordable price, it would already have been implemented. But this argument is analogous to the joke about the person who does not pick up a $100 bill from the sidewalk because if it were real, someone would have already picked it up; or akin to an entrepreneur who abandons a good business idea because if it were really sound, it would have been done earlier.

The reality is that we often underestimate the benefits which accrue in the future, especially when these are compared to immediate benefits. When faced with two future options — say receiving $10 in 14 days' time or $11 in 15 days — people usually apply appropriately low discount rates and choose the latter option of waiting an additional day. This implies that their implicit one-day discount rate is lower than 20% — which is also what market interest rates would predict. But when they are faced with $10 today and $11 tomorrow, people's discount rates often shoot up dramatically, and they favour $10 today instead. This choice implies that their discount rate between today and tomorrow is now more than 20%, which means that they must be compensated by more than 20% to wait an additional day. This inconsistency in discount rates — low when choosing between two future options but very high between today and the future — is known as hyperbolic discounting. It manifests itself in people often choosing short-term gratification over larger, longer term rewards. The reality of hyperbolic discounting goes against the standard economic assumption that people have stable and consistent discount rates.

Energy efficiency is often held back by people's tendency to discount distant benefits excessively. The rewards from adopting energy-efficient measures — the savings in our electricity bills over the longer term — are heavily discounted when weighed against immediate costs. Ruderman *et al.* (1987) found that consumers applied implicit discount rates of 80% or greater, when deciding whether to invest in energy-efficient water heaters, refrigerators and freezers over the 1972–1980 period. In the case of gas water heaters, the implicit discount rates were 500–800%, which means that even efficiency measures with a payback period of only about 5 months were not being adopted.

People used to paying under $1 for an incandescent light bulb are often unwilling to pay $6 for a compact fluorescent lamp which lasts more than six times longer and saves more in electricity and replacements than it costs. It is a good deal but it sounds like too much money to pay upfront.

Myopia and high discount rates suggest that it often makes sense for governments to introduce mandatory energy performance standards to remove the most inefficient appliances from the market and to preclude bad choices in the first place. In Singapore, the Minimum Energy Performance Standards (MEPS) will be implemented for household air conditioners and refrigerators in 2011, with an expected collective consumer energy savings of S$20 million annually for all appliances phased out by the scheme. Similarly, the European Union (EU) has banned energy-inefficient fridges and freezers from 1 July 2010 and laid down energy efficiency requirements for industrial motors, circulators and televisions. The European Commission has calculated that this will reduce EU energy consumption by around 190 terawatt-hours per year by 2020, equivalent to the total power used by Austria and Sweden (EUROPA 2009). These energy savings would probably not be realised without the outright ban.

The Psychology of Unsustainable Consumption

Psychology tells us a lot about how we can encourage environmentally sustainable behaviour. Unfortunately, the way countries currently grow is far from sustainable. The environment cannot absorb further increases in greenhouse gases, while the earth's mineral and agricultural resources are finite. The World Wildlife

Fund (WWF) analysed data relating the quality of life in each country to the size of the ecological footprint per capita. To measure the quality of life, it used the UN Human Development Index (HDI) which combines life expectancy, education and GDP per capita. No country bar one (Cuba) combines a good quality of life (above the WWF threshold of 0.8 on the HDI) with a sustainable ecological footprint (WWF 2006).

This problem of unsustainable consumption (of the kind seen in rich countries — where the US produces 15 times more carbon per person compared to India) is rooted in consumerism — a sociocultural pressure to consume, which makes it hard to contain economic activity within sustainable levels.

In developed countries, a great deal of what drives consumption is status competition and having to run to keep up with everyone else. None of us wants to appear inferior. Once we have enough of the necessities of life, it is the relativities that matter. In one experiment, people were asked whether they would prefer to be less well-off than others in a rich society, or have a much lower income in a poorer society but be better off than others. 50% of the participants thought they would trade as much as half of their real income if they could live in a society in which they would be better off than others (Layard 2005).

Some writers have also suggested that inequality increases this status competition, and ratchets up the competitive pressure to consume (Frank 2007). When people live in more unequal and individualistic societies, they use possessions to make a positive impression and to avoid appearing inadequate in the eyes of others. Goods are produced and consumed for what they confer in status and prestige, more than for their intrinsic usefulness.

We should not however assume we are stuck with high levels of self-interested consumerism, individualism and materialism that will defeat any attempt to develop sustainable economic systems. These are not fixed expressions of human nature. Rather, they reflect the dynamics of the societies in which we find ourselves.

In fact, research suggests that societies that are more cohesive and have higher levels of trust are more likely to foster the public spiritedness and concern for others that ultimately form the basis for environmentally sound behaviours (Wilkinson and Pickett 2009). The long-term success of policies to reduce our environmental impacts (from littering to resource conservation) will depend on this wider sense of social responsibility, cooperation and public spiritedness.

Conclusion

Clearly, a deeper understanding of the psychology of why people engage in environmentally friendly behaviours can help governments devise intelligent policies to promote sustainability. Sound environmental policies need to go beyond the conventional economist's approach of taxing negative environmental externalities (like pollution and carbon emissions) and subsidising positive ones (like recycling).

Behavioural economics offers a practical guide for formulating environmental policies that are more likely to be effective and widely accepted. Beyond ensuring that our environmental policies are compatible with incentives, environmental policymakers should also identify ways in which they can be compatible with human psychology. This requires them to take into account people's image motivations, to structure incentives in a way that accounts for their loss aversion, to make intelligent use of their availability bias, to be conscious of how mental accounting might affect their receptivity to environmental taxes, and to adjust for their tendency to discount the future excessively. Equally important, environmental policymakers should also be cognisant of the relationship between the culture of consumerism and sustainability and how our pursuit of relative position can impede the quest for sustainable development.

References

EUROPA (2009). "Commission adopts four ecodesign regulations that will save the equivalent power consumption of Austria and Sweden", press release, 22 July, viewed 10 December 2010, http://europa.eu/rapid/pressReleasesAction.do?reference=IP/09/1179

Frank, Robert (2007). *Falling Behind: How Rising Inequality Harms the Middle Class*. University of California Press.

Heffner, Reid, Kenneth Kurani and Thomas Turrentine (2005). "Effects of Vehicle Image in Gasoline-Hybrid Electric Vehicles." *21st Worldwide Battery, Hybrid, and Fuel Cell Electric Vehicle Symposium and Exhibition (EVS-21)*, 2–6 April.

Kahneman, Daniel and Amos Tversky (1979). "Prospect Theory: An Analysis of Decision Under Risk." *Econometrica*, Vol. 47, No. 2, pp. 263–292.

Krugman, Paul (2010). "The Finite World", *The New York Times*, 26 December, viewed 4 March 2011, http://www.nytimes.com/2010/12/27/opinion/27krugman.html

Layard, Richard (2005). *Happiness: Lessons From a New Science*. The Penguin Press.

Local Government Association (2009). "Zero Waste Places", viewed 10 December 2010, http://www.lga.gov.uk/lga/core/page.do?pageId=1212879

Ruderman, Henry, Mark Levine and James McMahon (1987). "The Behavior of the Market for Energy Efficiency in Residential Appliances including Heating and Cooling Equipment." *The Energy Journal*, Vol. 8, No. 1, pp. 101–124.

Wilkinson, Richard and Kate Pickett (2009). *The Spirit Level: Why Greater Equality Makes Societies Stronger*. The Penguin Press.

World Wildlife Fund (2006). "The Footprint and Human Development." *Living Planet Report 2006*, p. 19.

CHAPTER 5

PROMOTING COMPETITION IN ELECTRICITY RETAIL: INSIGHTS FROM BEHAVIOURAL ECONOMICS

Eugene TOH and Vivienne LOW

Introduction

Since 1995, the electricity industry in Singapore has been privatised and progressively deregulated. The driving force in this journey has been the belief — consistent with standard economic principles — that a competitive energy market will be more efficient as profit-maximising producers strive to reduce production costs and compete for customers. Any remaining monopoly power in the market can be controlled through proper design of the market structure as well as rules that prevent anti-competitive behaviours.

The journey towards full competition in the electricity industry began in 1995 when the government corporatised its electricity and gas holdings. In 2000, the government went a step further and separated utilities into two segments: the natural monopolies (the electricity grid and gas pipeline companies) and the contestable markets (the generation companies and retailers). The latter segment was opened up for competition, and the Energy Market Authority (EMA) was established to regulate the electricity industry.

In 2003, the government set up a wholesale market where generation companies would compete with one another to sell electricity to the grid. As predicted by standard economics, the introduction of competition has led to lower costs, both from more efficient operations as well as cheaper fuel alternatives such as natural gas.[1] This switch has helped to moderate the rise in electricity tariffs at a time of sharply rising fuel oil prices.

As for the electricity retail market, this was liberalised in phases from 2003, beginning with the largest consumers. By 2007, about 10,000 accounts, representing about 75% of the electricity consumed in Singapore, could choose from competing electricity retailers. EMA's goal is to eventually extend retail competition to the remaining 25%, or 1.2 million domestic or small commercial consumers.

On the whole, retail competition has benefited consumers in Singapore. Besides the price moderation discussed above, electricity retailers have also innovated and introduced new products as they competed for customers. These include fixed price contracts that help consumers to hedge against price volatility and value-added services such as online portals that allow consumers to view and manage their consumption on a real-time basis. Similar consumer benefits have also been demonstrated in the liberalised energy markets of the United Kingdom (Ofgem 2007) and Australia (Australian Energy Market Commission 2008a and 2008b).

The drive for full retail competition in Singapore is taking place alongside the emergence of smart grid technologies. Both trends have the potential to advance energy efficiency and conservation in Singapore and to help consumers make better electricity consumption decisions.

This chapter looks at how behavioural economics can provide useful ideas for energy regulators in promoting competition in the electricity retail market. The central argument is that while full retail competition will give consumers more choice over their electricity retailers and plans, this alone is not sufficient to ensure good consumer outcomes. By providing insights on how consumers decide when faced with complicated choices, in which the information needed is often not salient or timely, behavioural economics

---

[1] By 2009, 81% of electricity generated in Singapore came from burning natural gas, with another 15% from fuel oil. This compares with only 18.5% natural gas and 77.3% fuel oil in 2001 (Energy Market Authority of Singapore).

provides useful inputs to energy policymakers, particularly on how to structure choices in a way that improves individual consumption decisions and enhances overall energy efficiency.

Insights from Behavioural Economics

Providing Information to Overcome the Status Quo Bias

An important consideration when implementing full retail competition is to determine how consumers choose their retailers and pricing plans. One model is the "big bang" approach, which is to open up the entire customer market at one go for retail competition. Since consumers may not actively exercise choice, this approach requires the authorities to assign default retailers and plans to consumers. Behavioural economics predicts that many consumers are then unlikely to switch out of the default plan for them, even if it is in their best interests to do so — an effect known as the status quo bias. In their paper "Behavioural Science and Energy Policy", Allcott and Mullainathan (2010) provide possible reasons for this bias: procrastination, the endowment effect (people's implicit preference for their existing plans), and the costs of acquiring information about alternative options. Status quo bias contradicts the predictions of conventional economics which predicts that consumers will switch as long as switching is cheap and saves them money. It can result in markets with a low overall churn rate (i.e. the rate of consumers switching retailers), which in turn could undermine the efficiency of a fully competitive electricity market.

Are there ways to counter people's status quo bias? A smart metering trial conducted by the EMA for about 400 customers in 2009 provides evidence for cautious optimism. In this trial, participants were offered a choice of packages that reflects how retailers may price their packages in a competitive environment (see Exhibit 1).

Behavioural economics suggests that participants would likely stay with their existing plan, due either to the status quo bias or to consumers' unfamiliarity and fears that they could be made worse

	Peak Electricity Price (7 am–7 pm)	Off-peak Electricity Price (7 pm–7 am)
Status Quo (Current Regulated Tariff)	25 cents/kWh	25 cents/kWh
Pricing Plan A	30 cents/kWh	20 cents/kWh
Pricing Plan B	20 cents/kWh	35 cents/kWh

Exhibit 1:   Packages offered to participants in EMA smart metering trial.

off if they switched. To address this, the trial included a "recommended offer" package that was made available to all participants. The system would calculate the least-cost option based on that particular household's consumption profile from the previous month and recommend the appropriate package to them. For example, the system would recommend Pricing Plan A to a household which consumes most of its electricity in the evenings. This feature was made possible by smart meters installed in the homes of the trial participants, which recorded household consumption in half-hourly intervals and enabled the system to determine the "recommended offer".

As a result of this feature, about 95% of the participants opted for either Pricing Plan A or B, instead of staying with the status quo plan. This suggests that providing a "recommended offer" option, made possible by smart metering technologies that identify the plan that is most suitable for the user, may be sufficient to overcome consumers' status quo bias. Even consumers who may not be well-informed of the options available to them might switch if they are told that they would enjoy savings under a different plan.

Factoring Loss Aversion in the Design of Pricing Schemes

Governments and utility companies around the world have begun to provide electricity consumers with the means to change their consumption patterns so as to achieve a more efficient power system. In particular, they seek to shift consumers' electricity demand away from the day (when system demand typically peaks) to the nights (when system demand is lower). Such a shift would allow power companies to run fewer peaking plants during the day, thereby lowering the overhead costs of the power system and achieving savings for consumers. One of the most important ways of achieving this is to differentiate electricity prices by timing, through charging higher prices for electricity in peak periods of the day and lower prices for periods at night when demand for electricity is lower.

In designing pricing schemes, behavioural economics suggests that we should be mindful of people's loss aversion. Conventional economics says that people are symmetric in their responses to gains and losses of the same size. In other words, a person's increased utility as a result of gaining $X is the same as his reduced utility from losing $X.

However, behavioural economics suggests that consumers tend to be loss averse, also known as the phenomenon in which the "disutility of giving up an object is greater than the utility associated with acquiring it" (Kahneman *et al.* 1991, p. 194). In other words, people value losses more than improvements or gains of the same magnitude.

This loss aversion effect was vividly demonstrated in the Smart Meter Pilot Program conducted by PowerCentsDC, a power utility company in the United States. In the pilot, consumers were placed (without choice) on a variety of price plans: a critical peak pricing (CPP) scheme in which consumers were charged significantly higher during peak periods of the year, a critical peak rebate (CPR) scheme in which consumers earned rebates for reduced consumption below a certain baseline during critical periods, and an hourly pricing (HP) scheme in which consumers were charged the hourly prices of the electricity wholesale market. Details and the results of the trial are shown in Exhibits 2a and 2b respectively.

While the CPP and CPR pricing schemes provided identical monetary incentives for consumers to use electricity during off-peak periods, the results were significantly different. Consumers under the CPP responded more positively (i.e. they switched more of their usage from peak to off-peak) than those placed under the

Price Plan	Description	Example Prices per kWh	High Price/Rebate Event Hours
CPP	Slight discount during 8700 hours per year; much higher price during critical peaks (60 hours per year)	Critical peak: about 75¢; most times: 10.9¢	2 pm-6 pm summer weekdays (12 events per summer); 6 am-8 am and 6 pm-8 pm winter weekdays (3 events per winter)
CPR	Rebates earned for reduction below baseline during critical peaks	Rebate: about - 75¢; most times: 11¢	Same as for CPP
HP	Prices change hourly, following wholesale prices	Range from 1¢ to 37¢	High prices typically occur on summer weekday afternoons and winter mornings/evenings

Exhibit 2a: Design of the trial by PowerCentsDC: Electricity pricing plans.
Source: PowerCentsDC Final Report (2010).

Price Plan	Peak Reduction – Summer	Peak Reduction – Winter
CPP	34%	13%
CPR	13%	5%
HP	4%	2%

Exhibit 2b: Results of the trial by PowerCentsDC: Average percentage energy usage reduction during critical peak hours (comparing treatment and control group).
Source: PowerCentsDC Final Report (2010).

CPR. People are much more likely to switch from peak to off-peak usage when they are under a plan that charges them a high price for peak usage than if they are under one which gives them a high rebate for switching. This is consistent with what loss aversion predicts — that people try to avoid losses more than they try to pursue gains.

This example suggests that policymakers face an important trade-off when designing such dynamic pricing schemes: a scheme that leans on "carrots" or rebates to encourage people to switch may be more popular, but "using the stick" or appealing to people's loss aversion may achieve a better policy outcome. Finding the balance will then be a challenge for decision makers in regulatory agencies and utility companies alike.

Increasing Energy Efficiency through Saliency and Social Norms

Promoting energy efficiency and energy conservation among consumers is another important policy objective of many governments. While the power system has traditionally been built around a "supply follows demand" approach, where generation capacity is typically invested ahead of demand, studies have suggested that it is cheaper to invest in energy efficiency than to invest in energy generation, such as building a new power plant (Lovins 2007).

Standard economics suggests that to achieve higher levels of energy efficiency, energy prices will have to be raised (for instance, through an energy tax). Higher prices create a stronger incentive for consumers to reduce their usage, while signalling to energy companies to develop and implement energy efficiency solutions. Conventional economics also assumes that individual consumers are rational beings who optimise their consumption regardless of how the information is presented.

Behavioural economics suggests an alternative approach. It argues that presenting information that is salient to the choices and framing that information appropriately can go a long way in influencing consumers' behaviour. Allcott and Mullainathan (2010, p. 3) also suggest that "appealing to social norms can be another powerful non-price behavioural lever. People may conform to others' behaviour because they believe in [the] wisdom of crowds, i.e. that others took an action because they had more or different information about its benefits, or because there is some external approbation or inner comfort from conformity".

Currently, some aspects of this are already employed in the promotion of energy conservation in Singapore. SP Services, which manages the utilities accounts of all households, provides information in utility bills on the household's electricity consumption in relation to similar households in Singapore (see Exhibit 3). The intent is to nudge consumers who are consuming above the national average for their housing type towards reducing their energy use.

Bar Graph for Past Consumption

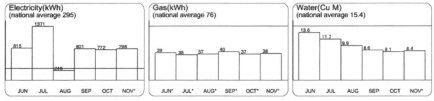

Consumption based on estimated reading

—— *National average consumption for your house type*

Exhibit 3:   Extract from sample utilities bill displaying relative consumption of electricity, gas and water.

Source: SP Services.

In an experiment, Cialdini *et al.* (2008) studied the impact of different messages to encourage hotel guests to reuse their towels. Various messages such as "Save the Environment", "Preserve Resources for the Future", and "Partner with the Hotel to Save the Environment" were printed on cards which were visible to hotel guests. The outcome of this study was that the card with the message "Join Your Fellow Citizens in Helping to Save the Environment", which provided the information that 75% of hotel guests reused their towels, increased towel reuse by the largest margin of 39.2% — a clear indication that appealing to social norms can make a stronger impact on consumers' behaviour. Thaler and Sunstein (2008) in their book *Nudge: Improving Decisions about Health, Wealth and Happiness,* termed such conformity with social norms as the herd phenomenon, or the tendency of people to care about what others think of them.

Another barrier to energy conservation is that consumers find it difficult to know how much energy they are using at any point in time. This is exacerbated by the typical time lag of about a month between their actual consumption and their receipt of the monthly utility bills. This lag reduces the immediacy and saliency of the information, and weakens the motivation for consumers to change their habits.

Technological advances such as smart meters make it possible to provide consumers with more information and control over their energy consumption patterns. The question of interest to energy regulators is whether making available real-time information

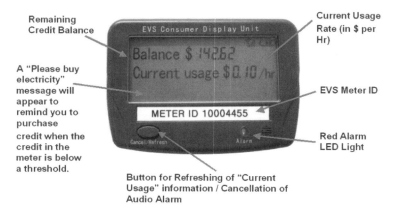

Remaining Credit Balance

A "Please buy electricity" message will appear to remind you to purchase credit when the credit in the meter is below a threshold.

Current Usage Rate (in $ per Hr)

EVS Meter ID

Red Alarm LED Light

Button for Refreshing of "Current Usage" information / Cancellation of Audio Alarm

Exhibit 4: In-home display unit providing real-time consumption information.

Source: Energy Market Authority.

enabled by these technologies (see Exhibit 4) can promote energy conservation and modify usage patterns to a degree significant enough to justify their large-scale deployment.

How might the information be presented in a way that impacts energy consumption levels? What is the right level of detail? And are the changes to consumer behaviour permanent and sustainable? Consider the following options to frame the consumption information which households can see on their in-home display units that provide "live" information on their electricity usage (see Exhibit 5).

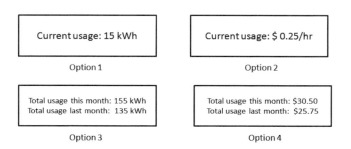

Current usage: 15 kWh

Option 1

Current usage: $ 0.25/hr

Option 2

Total usage this month: 155 kWh
Total usage last month: 135 kWh

Option 3

Total usage this month: $30.50
Total usage last month: $25.75

Option 4

Exhibit 5: Framing electricity consumption information.

Source: Energy Market Authority.

Behavioural economics suggests that showing consumers their usage in monetary terms (Options 2 and 4) will have a greater impact than showing them the units of electricity used (Options 1 and 3), as the former makes more intuitive sense. It also suggests that showing consumers their consumption level on a real-time basis (Option 2) may be more effective than showing them their cumulative usage over the month (Option 4), since the former provides current, rather than backward-looking information.

Another possibility is to make use of ambient displays which alert consumers of high levels of electricity consumption through changes in colours or light displays (Darby 2006). Martinez and Geltz (2005) described an experiment where electricity consumers were provided with a device called an "Energy Orb", a globe that changes its colour according to the time-of-use tariff in operation. The study indicated that the flashing alert of higher tariffs resulted in higher overall savings and more load-shifting, strengthening the case for visual cues as long as they are cost-effective.

The key challenge then in designing any electricity information system is to identify the signals that are the most effective in inducing behavioural change, all the while bearing in mind the risk of "information overload". Psychologists have documented a reduced sense of individual efficacy when people are overwhelmed by the choices presented to them. When consumers are faced with too many choices, such as too many pricing plans or too much information and fine print, they are often paralysed by confusion and indecision and end up not taking action at all. The key takeaway for regulators and utility companies is to calibrate the number of choices and the amount of information to provide consumers. They should also ensure that the choices presented to consumers are clear and easy to understand.

Singapore's Intelligent Energy System Pilot

In Singapore, full retail competition is still work-in-progress. The eventual aim is to give consumers greater say over their electricity retailers and pricing plans and to harness the full range of available technologies to improve Singapore's energy efficiency.

Since 2010, the government has been pilot-testing the Intelligent Energy System (IES). Involving 4,500 residential, commercial and industrial customers, the pilot aims to provide consumers with more information, choice and control over their electricity usage. For instance, smart meters will provide consumers with real-time information on consumption and prices, giving them greater control over their energy consumption decisions, for example by shifting their demand from costly peak periods to cheaper off-peak periods. The ideas that are being tested range from different pricing models to the design of smart display units to be installed in consumers' homes. Through the IES pilot, EMA will also be able to assess how to apply the ideas from behavioural economics to shape consumer behaviour and increase energy efficiency.

Conclusion

While standard economics still underpins the formulation of energy policies in Singapore, behavioural economics provides additional insights in explaining consumer behaviours and in formulating energy policies. The introduction of full retail competition will increase choice for consumers but simply expanding the range of options may not result in good decisions by consumers. The technological advancements that the IES offers will allow utility companies and energy regulators to provide salient and timely information to consumers. By combining the insights of behavioural economics with these new technology solutions, policymakers can devise creative measures that help consumers save money and promote energy efficiency.

References

Allcott, Hunt and Sendil Mullainathan (2010). "Behavioral Science and Energy Policy", viewed 22 January 2011, http://web.mit.edu/allcott/www/Allcott%20and%20Mullainathan%202010%20-%20Behavioral%20Science%20and%20Energy%20Policy.pdf

Australian Energy Market Commission (2008a). "Review of the Effectiveness of Competition in Electricity and Gas Retail Markets in South Australia." *Second Final Report.*

Australian Energy Market Commission (2008b). "Review of the Effectiveness of Competition in Electricity and Gas Retail Markets in Victoria." *Second Final Report.*

Cialdini, Robert, Noah Goldstein and Vladas Griskevicius (2008). "A Room with a Viewpoint: Using Social Norms to Motivate Environmental Conservation in Hotels." *Journal of Consumer Research,* Vol. 35, pp. 472–482.

Darby, Sarah (2006). "The Effectiveness of Feedback on Energy Consumption: A Review for DEFRA of the Literature on Metering, Billing and Direct Displays." Environmental Change Institute. University of Oxford, viewed 10 August 2011, http://www.eci.ox.ac.uk/research/energy/downloads/smart-metering-report.pdf

Kahneman, Daniel, Jack Knetsch and Richard Thaler (1991). "Anomalies: The Endowment Effect, Loss Aversion, and Status Quo Bias." *The Journal of Economics Perspectives,* Vol. 5, No. 1, Winter, pp. 193–206.

Lovins, Amory (2007). "Advanced Energy Efficiency: Implementation." Stanford University, Civil and Environmental Engineering Department.

Martinez, Mark and Cristine Geltz (2005). "Utilizing a Pre-Attentive Technology for Modifying Customer Energy Usage." *Proceedings, European Council for an Energy-Efficient Economy,* 30 May–4 June.

Office of the Gas and Electricity Markets (2007). "Domestic Retail Market Report, June 2007", prepared by Office of Gas and Electricity Markets (Ofgem), United Kingdom, viewed 22 January 2011, http://www.ofgem.gov.uk/Markets/RetMkts/Compet/Documents1/DRMR%20March%202007doc%20v9%20-%20FINAL.pdf

PowerCentsDC Final Report (2010). *PowerCentsDC^{TM} Program Final Report*, prepared by eMeter Strategic Consulting for the Smart Meter Pilot Program, Inc, September 2010.

Thaler, Richard and Cass Sunstein (2008). *Nudge: Improving Decisions about Health, Wealth and Happiness*. Yale University Press.

CHAPTER 6

DISCRETIONARY TRANSFERS: PROVIDING FISCAL SUPPORT IN A BEHAVIOURALLY COMPATIBLE WAY

Pamela QIU and TAN Li San[1]

"We don't assume that people will take a completely long-term enlightened perspective...We are prepared to subsidise wealth, but not incomes...[to allow citizens] to feel that they own the wealth rather than to give [them] an allowance or a salary."

Lee Hsien Loong (2003)

Introduction

In the post-WWII era, most governments in developed economies implemented demand management policies to moderate business cycles, maintain full employment and fine-tune the real economy. Fiscal policy was used in an activist way to counteract the ups and downs of the real economy: governments increased spending and cut taxes in a slowdown and reversed these during the recovery (or at least, they were supposed to do so). The experience of stagflation in the 1970s, the monetarist revolution in macroeconomics, and the

[1] The authors would like to thank their former colleagues at the Ministry of Finance (MOF) for their valuable inputs and suggestions. We are particularly grateful to Lim Siong Guan, Lam Chuan Leong, Teo Ming Kian, Ng Wai Choong, Chua Geok Wah, Donald Low, Lawrence Wong, Lee Tung Jean, Musa Fazal, Ong Kian Ann, Jane Lim, Liu Feng-yuan and Gloria Chung for their comments and suggestions. The opinions expressed in this chapter represent the views of the authors and should not be attributed to MOF.

practical difficulties of implementing counter-cyclical fiscal policies combined to make fiscal policymakers more restrained in their use of fiscal stabilisation policies.

From the 1980s onwards, the emphasis shifted towards the use of interest rates to manage business cycle fluctuations. Governments also targeted inflation control, instead of full employment, as the object of macroeconomic policy. While governments still pursued counter-cyclical fiscal policies, they did so more sparingly and only in specific circumstances such as when interest rates were already very low (Feldstein 2002; Blinder 2006). Instead of fine-tuning the real economy, fiscal policy should be aimed at balancing budgets over the business cycle, maintaining predictability and credibility, and supporting growth over the medium term.

As part of this new consensus on macroeconomic policy, governments should rely less on discretionary fiscal measures and more on automatic stabilisers, or the institutional mechanisms that stabilise an economy automatically. For example, in a recession, the government automatically collects less tax revenues and spends more on jobless benefits. These help to support private consumption and aggregate demand without the need for discretionary policy measures. In a recovery, the opposite effects kick in, reining in spending and inflationary pressures, again without the need for deliberate fiscal policy changes.

The 2008/2009 financial crisis has revived the debate on whether fiscal policy should pursue short-term stabilisation objectives and on the appropriate balance between automatic stabilisers and discretionary measures. At the height of the crisis, governments around the world scrambled to put together large fiscal stimulus programmes. In addition to enhancing their automatic stabilisers (such as extensions to unemployment insurance), many governments also introduced temporary fiscal measures to offset the falls in private investment and consumption. The use of discretionary fiscal measures to stabilise the economy became popular once again.

In Singapore, discretionary fiscal measures have been an increasingly important component of fiscal policy since the 1990s. Funded mainly out of budget surpluses, annual spending on such discretionary transfers (commonly referred to as "special trans-fers") has varied substantially between 0.04% and 2.3% of GDP since 1992, or between S$52 million in 1998 and S$3.5 billion in 2001. Besides counter-cyclical objectives, Singapore's discretionary fiscal transfers serve at least two other purposes: to help Singaporeans build up their savings and to offset increases in Singapore's broad-based consumption tax (also known as the Goods and Services Tax or GST).

This chapter discusses the design and implementation of Singapore's discretionary transfers — in the context of both the international experience as well as the government's policy objectives. We first review the international experience of how discretionary transfers might provide counter-cyclical support. We then describe how behavioural considerations have shaped the design of discretionary fiscal transfers in Singapore.

An Overview of the International Experience

The difficulties of practising counter-cyclical fiscal policies have been a staple of macroeconomics textbooks for decades (Auerbach 2002). Milton Friedman (1953), for example, pointed to the time lags in the implementation of discretionary fiscal policy and the uncertainties regarding the nature and magnitude of the private sector's response to such changes. The Lucas Critique (1976) high-lighted the difficulties of predicting firm and household behaviour to policy changes on the basis of past patterns since their expectations are constantly revised in light of new information. The evidence on the efficacy of discretionary fiscal policies for macro-economic stabilisation remains mixed: at best, the results suggest positive, but limited, effectiveness (Auerbach 2002; Blanchard and Perotti 2002; Perotti 2002).

To a large extent, the effectiveness of discretionary fiscal policies depends on timing and political will. While governments find it rela-tively easy to increase spending in response to an economic contraction, they often find it difficult to reverse the spending increases when macroeconomic conditions improve. This asymmetry in discretionary fiscal measures — which results in public spending and the government's debt burden creeping upwards over time — is the main argument for relying more on automatic stabilisers instead. Because they are more likely to operate symmetrically, building automatic stabilisers into the fiscal system is arguably a better way of stabilising the economy.

The effectiveness of automatic stabilisers also depends on, among other things, the size of government, the composition of government revenue and expenditures, and the progressiveness of the tax-and-transfers system. These factors vary across countries and over time. A study by the Organisation for Economic Co-operation and Development (OECD) estimates that in the 1990s, automatic stabilisers (on average) reduced cyclical fluctuations in rich countries by a quarter, but also that there were significant variations in the size of these effects. In countries with large government sectors such as Finland and Denmark, they reduced output volatility by more than half; where taxes and spending are lower relative to GDP, such as in Japan and the United States, their effects were significantly smaller (Van den Noord 2000).

The 2008/2009 crisis prompted governments in many G20 countries to ring-fence and extend their existing social protection programmes. In the United States for instance, almost 40% of the resources foreseen in the American Recovery and Reinvestment Act were directed at increasing spending on existing programmes such as pensions, education, health, unemployment insurance, social assistance, and tax cuts for low-income and vulnerable people (Congressional Budget Office 2009). These measures represented enhancements to existing programmes and did not produce structural changes in the US social protection system (Burtless 2009). Both in the United States and elsewhere, there were also special, one-time payments to low-income households. Other measures included temporary exemptions from social security contributions either to reduce costs for employers and so stimulate employment or to raise the net earnings of low-income workers. Canada, China, Germany and Japan all lowered contribution rates and granted exemptions to unemployment insurance contributions.

Thus far, there is little consensus among economists regarding the effectiveness of the 2008/2009 fiscal stimulus packages. An OECD (2009) report estimates that for the average OECD country, such stimulus packages increased output by only 0.5%. Only in the US and Australia were the estimated effects on GDP greater than 1%.

Despite the lack of consensus on the efficacy of the 2009 fiscal stimulus measures, most economists and policymakers agree that discretionary fiscal measures are more effective if they are accompanied by credible commitments to scale them back when the economy recovers. This underlines the importance of strengthening medium-term fiscal frameworks that ensure fiscal sustainability and support long-term growth.

Automatic Stabilisers and Discretionary Transfers in Singapore

In Singapore, one would expect automatic stabilisers to have a relatively limited impact during a downturn. Unlike most OECD countries with large redistributive fiscal systems, Singapore has one of the lowest levels of income and wealth taxes in the world. Government spending as a share of national income — at 16–18% of GDP — is also extremely low by international standards. This means that automatic increases in government spending when the economy contracts start from a very low base. This is compounded by the fact that Singapore lacks comprehensive social safety nets which in a downturn would automatically increase public spending.

Partly as a result of relatively weak automatic stabilisers, the Singapore government has begun to rely more on discretionary fiscal measures to cope with a volatile economic environment. The economic contractions in 2001 and 2003 forced Singapore's Ministry of Finance (MOF) to examine how activist fiscal policies can help to cushion the effects of a recession. Balancing the budget over the business cycle — as opposed to balancing it every year — became MOF's new mantra as it ran sizeable deficits in FY2001 and

FY2003. At the same time, given the open nature of Singapore's economy, the impact of counter-cyclical fiscal policy is likely to be quite limited compared to economies that are less exposed to trade. This is because much of the additional spending by government would "leak out" via increased imports. Estimates for Singapore's Keynesian expenditure multiplier are typically very low, ranging from between 0.56 and 0.61 (Abeysinghe and Choy 2007), suggesting that fiscal pump-priming measures aimed at increasing aggregate demand are likely to be of limited effectiveness.

Standard economic theory also suggests that social transfers should be provided in cash rather than in kind. Cash does not constrain the recipient's consumption choices and gives him the flexibility to allocate resources according to his preferences. Furthermore, neoclassical economic theory suggests that the most efficient way of redistributing wealth would be to give lower-income individuals lump sum transfers without prescribing or circumscribing how these transfers are used — whether for current consumption or saved for future needs.

Social spending in Singapore takes a contrary approach. The lion's share of social spending is not given as cash transfers but is provided in kind, especially in the areas of education, housing, healthcare and worker retraining. The only substantial and permanent cash transfer that the Singapore government provides is the wage supplement given to low-wage workers, the Workfare Income Supplement (WIS). Like the Earned Income Tax Credit in the United States and the Working Tax Credit in the United Kingdom, the WIS is aimed at supporting low-wage workers in employment. It is provided to Singaporean workers aged 35 and above earning below $1,700 per month.

The Singapore government's approach — of favouring in-kind subsidies over cash transfers and of enhancing the savings of Singaporeans rather than subsidising their consumption — reflects the belief that individuals are likely to have bounded self-control. They often place too high a value on present consumption and under-invest in areas that yield longer-term benefits. Faced with a (small) windfall gain, they are more likely to spend it immediately than to save it for the future, which suggests that they apply a much higher discount rate on future benefits.

Throughout the 1990s, Singapore enjoyed sustained fiscal surpluses which the government sought to return to Singaporeans in ways that were consistent with its approach to social spending. Surplus-sharing programmes during this decade typically took the form of one-off top-ups to the Central Provident Fund (CPF), Medisave and Edusave accounts of Singaporeans. The details of discretionary transfer programmes introduced between 1992 and 2009 are provided in the Appendix of this chapter. The measures in the 1990s reflected an emphasis on enhancing the savings of Singaporeans, rather than on subsidising current consumption.

Since the early 2000s, against the backdrop of a more volatile economic environment, the government's objectives in providing discretionary transfers have expanded in scope. Notably, discretionary transfers have come to play a more important role in providing counter-cyclical support for the economy. There has been a greater willingness by the government to run primary budget deficits and implement accommodative fiscal policies during periods of economic contraction.

How has the Singapore government designed its discretionary fiscal measures in light of its expanded objectives? The rest of this chapter discusses how Singapore's MOF has applied behavioural considerations in designing discretionary transfers to provide counter-cyclical support for the economy and to fulfil its other policy objectives.

Designing and Implementing the Right Discretionary Transfers

Behavioural Consideration 1: Correcting for the Lack of Self-Control

Conventional economic theories of consumption, such as the life-cycle hypothesis, typically assume that rational individuals will want to maintain consistent consumption levels and standards of living (Ando and Modigliani 1963). The permanent income hypothesis predicts that consumption is determined by one's lifetime income and is little affected by transitory changes in income (Friedman 1957). According to these theories, since "one-off" government transfers provide only a temporary boost in one's income and do not represent an increase in one's lifetime income, they should have no noticeable impact on one's consumption.

The Ricardian equivalence (Barro 1974) goes further. It predicts that individuals, anticipating a future increase in taxes, will respond to cash transfers from government by cutting back on their consumption. According to Barro, public borrowing is equivalent to taxation: any government stimulus financed by borrowing will be completely negated by increases in private saving, leaving output unchanged. The Ricardian Equivalence was widely used by conservative economists during the 2008/2009 crisis as an argument against the stimulus measures employed by governments around the world.

While elegant, these theories lack empirical support. The assumption that individuals are rational optimisers over long time horizons is seldom borne out in reality. For one, individuals have limited computational capacity and find it hard to estimate their lifetime incomes. Second, people have only bounded self-control and their consumption levels are influenced strongly by their preferences for short-term gratification. All this suggests that consumption is in fact highly correlated to one's current income and that people save with much less discipline than the permanent income hypothesis or the Ricardian Equivalence would have us believe.

The Singapore government's early approach to discretionary transfers reflects its view that individuals, left on their own, are unlikely to take a long-term view. Thus, rather than provide cash to Singaporeans, discretionary benefits up to the late 1990s were either distributed in kind (via rebates for utilities bills and service and conservancy charges) or channelled into various savings accounts for housing, retirement, education and healthcare purposes.

The 2001 New Singapore Shares (NSS) marked an important departure in the way government designed its discretionary transfers. The stated objective was to "help the lower-income group tide over the economic downturn". Under the NSS programme, shares that could be redeemed for cash were introduced for the first time. Designed to mimic savings bonds, larger allotments of NSS were given to lower-income Singaporeans and dividends were paid annually to those who held on to their shares (dividends were higher than market interest rate, guaranteed at 3% with additional "bonus payments" tied to GDP).[2] Furthermore, since the NSS were also "redeemable immediately for cash", Singaporeans could now choose between cash for immediate consumption or saving for future needs.

The government also took pains to highlight the opportunity costs of early redemption and encouraged citizens to hold on to their NSS. Those who held on to their NSS throughout the five-year scheme stood to receive maximum benefits, but Singaporeans on lower incomes (the target group that the government was seeking to assist) chose to cash out their NSS as soon as they could. In fact, the government had stipulated that only 50% of allotted NSS could be redeemed in the first year that the scheme was introduced (on 1 November 2001) to ensure that citizens would earn at least the first dividend payment (credited on 1 March 2002). However, by 31 December 2002, over 70% of Singaporeans had redeemed at least 75% of their allotments.

While the high percentage of early redemptions suggests that many Singaporeans may have required additional finances to help them cope with the recession, it is also the very outcome that would be predicted by behavioural economics and its depiction of individuals with strong present-biased preferences. Faced with a choice between current and deferred consumption, individuals often want to be compensated by a lot more than market interest rates to choose the latter. Citing existing literature and empirical

---

[2] At a cost of S$2.5 billion, the NSS was, at that time, the largest surplus-sharing programme in Singapore's fiscal history.

evidence, Beaulier and Caplan (2007) also argue that such biases and self-control problems are particularly pronounced among the poor. Neoclassical economists usually argue that this phenomenon can be explained by credit market imperfections. But as Richard Thaler (1992) points out, this argument lacks robustness as hyperbolic discounting persists even when individuals are not liquidity-constrained (for instance, when they have significant home equity or other liquid assets).

Behavioural Consideration 2: Avoiding a Sense of Entitlement

One of the Singapore government's key considerations when providing cash benefits is that they should not weaken incentives to work or create moral hazard. To avoid the public expectation that surplus-sharing programmes are the norm, the government has often taken pains to stress the discretionary or "one-off" nature of each initiative. These measures are also classified as "special transfers" in the Budget. The Minister for Finance's rationalisation of rebates in the 1992 Budget is typical:

> *Although our economy slowed down in 1991, we achieved a satisfactory growth rate of 6.7%.... The hard work and initiative on the part of our people contributed significantly to our success. I have therefore decided to encourage continued individual efforts by giving an across-the-board and one-off rebate of 5% for personal income tax.... For citizen householders who pay little or no income tax, the Government has decided to pay, on their behalf, the Service and Conservancy charges.... This is a one-off payment applicable to Singapore citizens only. It is the equivalent of the 5% income tax rebate.*

Finance Minister Dr Richard Hu (1992, p. 20)

No matter what form the transfers took — government fee rebates, savings top-ups or offsets for tax increases — the government always emphasised the unusual circumstances that Singapore faced on those occasions and the "one-off" nature of these budget giveaways. Discretionary transfers have been positioned as a response to exceptional circumstances. In a booming economy, they were presented as a way of distributing some of the surpluses made possible by economic growth. In a severe downturn (e.g. 2001 and 2009), they were framed as a way of helping Singaporeans cope with economic dislocation and uncertainty. In years when the GST rate was increased, the measures were presented as a way of helping citizens adjust to increased costs.

Even as the design and purpose of the discretionary transfers evolved, the government sought to ensure that the right economic incentives prevailed. Many behavioural experiments — dating back to Tversky and Kahneman (1974)[3] — have shown that people form preferences (or expectations) around reference points and that once a number (or idea) has been anchored in people's minds, they form their expectations or perceptions around it. In providing discretionary transfers, the Singapore government has tried to avoid creating a "typical package" that might become an anchor in people's minds and influence their expectations of what they would receive in subsequent years.

Specifically, this meant that the exact combination of discretionary benefits changed from year to year. The government has also varied the wealth and income cut-offs across programmes: sometimes the level of benefits was based on housing type, other times it was based on individual income. Such variations were

---

[3] The experiment asked volunteers a series of questions whose answers were in percentages — such as the percentage of African countries in the United Nations. A wheel with numbers from one to 100 was spun in front of them; they were then asked to say whether their answer was higher or lower than the number on the wheel and then asked to give their answer. These answers were strongly influenced by the randomly selected, irrelevant number on the wheel. The average guess when the wheel showed 10 was 25%; when it showed 65 it was 45%. In Richard Thaler's and Cass Sunstein's *Nudge* (2008), the authors highlight how the available donation options influence the generosity of donors. Charities will collect more if the options are $100, $250, $1,000 and $5,000, than if the options were $50, $75, $100 and $150.

important for another behavioural objective: they helped to ensure that people did not try to game the system in anticipation of securing larger benefits from future transfer programmes. Box 1 describes how the eligibility criteria for the major discretionary transfer programmes evolved in the last decade.

Box 1: Experimenting with the eligibility criteria

The set of criteria for the 2001 New Singapore Shares was particularly complex, with allotment being determined based on income level if the beneficiary was employed, the type of housing if he was unemployed, and both income and housing type for the self-employed. This led to a great deal of confusion and difficulties in communication.

The criteria for the 2002 Economic Restructuring Shares was greatly simplified to focus solely on the Annual Value (AV) of the beneficiary's residence. But with just 2 tiers of AV, 90% of the population received the higher amount. This in turn attracted feedback that payouts could have been better targeted.

Finally, the 2006 Progress Package payouts were settled on two fronts — annual income and AV. Since then, this formula has been replicated for subsequent programmes including GST Credits, Senior Citizens' Bonus and Growth Dividends.

Behavioural Consideration 3: Framing Benefits to Support Macroeconomic Objectives

The effectiveness of a fiscal stimulus is affected by how well it is timed and framed. While the importance of the first is well understood (the timing of the stimulus should closely match the timing of demand contraction in the economy), what is less appreciated is the extent to which framing might influence consumption. Small changes in the way stimulus packages are presented can affect whether they are saved or spent. For example, when tax cuts are framed as a "bonus" they are more likely to be spent than if they are framed as a "rebate". Despite being identical, a "bonus" describes a positive change from the status quo whereas a "rebate" describes a return to the status quo. As people are loss averse and have a psychological tendency to want to preserve the status quo, individuals are more likely to spend the tax cut if they perceive it as a gain (a "bonus") rather than a loss avoided (a "rebate").

Consistent with the Singapore government's emphasis on savings, "rebates", "offsets" and "credits" have formed a higher proportion of discretionary transfers, increasing their likelihood of being saved (or at least not spent until necessary). For instance, the 2006 and 2008 Growth Dividends — announced in years of good economic growth — were presented as dividends partly to encourage Singapore to save for an uncertain future.

The 2008/2009 economic crisis provides a good case study of Singapore's use of discretionary fiscal transfers to deal with an externally induced macroeconomic shock. As the effects of the global financial crisis began to be felt globally from late 2008 onwards, Singapore's fiscal policymakers were tasked to design and deliver a timely and sufficiently large fiscal stimulus package. The S$20.5 billion Resilience Package, unveiled in the January 2009 Budget Statement (brought forward from February in light of the urgency of dealing with the crisis) was aimed at stimulating growth and at supporting employment. The main approach was to help viable companies stay afloat and to save jobs. Consequently, the government's measures were focussed on businesses rather than individuals. Discretionary benefits to individuals were presented in the form of enhancements to existing schemes. These included increases in the GST Credits (which were introduced earlier in 2007 to compensate Singaporeans for the increase in the GST rate from 5% to 7%), income and property tax rebates, as well as utilities and service and conservancy charges (S&CC) rebates.

An alternative framing might have been to present the transfers as new, one-off "bonuses" instead of enhancements to existing schemes. This might have increased their likelihood of being spent, thereby positively impacting consumption.

Furthermore, instead of channelling the GST Credits automatically into individuals' bank accounts, could the government have done more to increase the saliency of these transfers to promote consumption? In other countries, time-limited shopping vouchers and eye-catching "cash for clunkers" programmes to spur immediate spending were a notable feature of their fiscal stimulus packages. That the Singapore government did not adopt these measures underscores its priorities, which were to help businesses reduce costs and save jobs (through the Jobs Credit Scheme[4]), and to ensure that credit was available to businesses (through the Special Risk-Sharing Initiative[5]). By increasing funding for training programmes, the government also provided incentives for businesses to send their workers for training instead of resorting to layoffs. Clearly, the Singapore government believed that it was more effective to minimise unemployment than to boost domestic consumption by way of direct cash transfers to citizens.

The government also had other reasons to enhance existing discretionary transfer programmes that it had previously committed to, rather than to roll out new, untested measures. First, given the urgency of the unfolding crisis, the government needed to be confident of both the timing and speed with which the discretionary transfers could reach citizens. The GST Credits and rebates

---

[4] The Jobs Credit scheme was part of the S$20.5 billion Resilience Package announced in Budget 2009 to help companies preserve jobs during the downturn. The scheme provides employers with a 12% cash grant on the first S$2,500 of wages for their Singaporean and permanent resident employees. It was introduced as a one-year scheme with four quarterly payments. In October 2009 however, the government announced that the scheme would be extended for another half a year, with two payments at stepped-down rates of 6% in March 2010 and 3% in June 2010.

[5] The Special Risk-Sharing Initiative (SRI) was the other major component of the Resilience Package. It sought to ensure that viable companies would continue to have access to bank credit. The SRI extended government support to mid-sized companies and involved government taking on a much larger share of the risks in credit extended by banks to companies. The SRI was introduced initially as a one-year scheme. In December 2009, the government announced that it would be extended for another year in 2010 on revised terms.

framework were tried-and-tested mechanisms which the government could readily and quickly implement with minimal administrative hassle.

Second, there were calls from some segments to cut the GST rate temporarily as a relief measure. The government's decision to increase GST Credits instead would have a stronger impact on consumption because one-off gains are more likely to be spent than tax savings. Furthermore, the GST Credits and rebates were weighted heavily in favour of the poor. This meant that they were a more efficient and targeted way of helping lower-income groups than an across-the-board cut in the GST. Lower-income individuals have higher propensities to consume — especially on domestically produced goods and services — so the multiplier effect was also likely to be greater.

Behavioural Consideration 4: Mental Accounting

The standard economic advice regarding tax rebates or benefits is that these should be given as a one-off, single lump sum. Not only does this cut down on implementation and transaction costs, the bigger sum of money also increases the likelihood of people spending it.

The behavioural reality however, is that the relationship between large windfalls and increased spending is not so straightforward. As proposed by Thaler (1999), people put different windfall gains in different "mental accounts" — for example, a "current income account" which is distinct from a "wealth account". Depending on which account the windfall gains are put into, they are either spent immediately or saved for the future. As people tend to consume from current income flows and leave perceived wealth alone, they are more likely to spend it if they think of the windfall as current income and more likely to save it if they perceive it as wealth. In other words, individuals have a higher marginal propensity to consume out of their "income" rather than "wealth" accounts.

The size of the windfall gain relative to income also matters. Empirical studies have shown that as the size of the windfall increases, the marginal propensity to consume out of that windfall decreases significantly; the studies also cite that the bigger the windfall is relative to regular income, the more likely it is to be saved (Landsberger 1966; Keeler *et al.* 1985).

This suggests that when the policy objective is to encourage consumption, as it is during downturns, a single large transfer is less effective than many, smaller transfers. The former is a larger windfall gain relative to income, so individuals are more likely to see it as gains in wealth that should be saved. Conversely, individuals are more likely to think of smaller multiple transfers as gains in income — or even "petty cash" — especially if the amount is small relative to their incomes. They would therefore be more likely to spend it. Empirically, there is evidence to support this hypothesis. For example, a recent experiment found that a tax refund delivered in monthly instalments is more likely to be spent than one delivered as a lump sum, an effect which diminishes as the refund size becomes a material amount. The study further concluded that lump sum distributions stimulate private saving more than monthly distributions do (Chambers and Spencer 2008; Shapiro and Slemrod 2003a; 2003b).

On hindsight, the Singapore government's decision to enhance the second instalment of the 2008 Growth Dividends to help citizens cope with inflation is consistent with the idea of mental accounting. By increasing the cash assistance provided as a single lump sum (rather than distributing it as separate, smaller payments), mental accounting predicts that this would induce smaller increases in spending and encourage more people to save the transfer. Given concerns that the economy was over-heating, this made macroeconomic sense too.

However, in deciding whether to provide benefits as a single lump sum or as multiple transfers, other factors apart from mental accounting should be taken into account. Policymakers may sometimes decide that the short-term impacts on consumption are less important than other objectives. For example, the 2003–2005 Economic Restructuring Shares (ERS) and the 2007–2010 GST Offset Package were intended to help citizens adjust to increases in the GST rate. Rather than provide counter-cyclical support, these transfers were intended to help citizens cope with price increases. Benefits from the ERS and GST Offset Package were hence distributed as annual instalments over three and four years, respectively, to help Singaporeans adjust to the new GST rates.

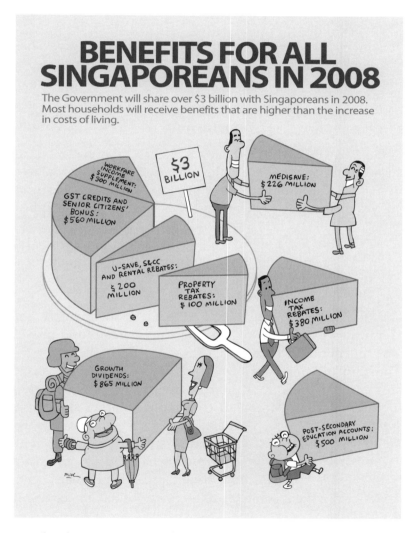

A poster that the government used to communicate various discretionary transfers to Singaporeans in 2008.

The administrative and political costs associated with multiple transfers are additional factors to consider. Politically, multiple transfers may be harder to roll back, precisely because people may come to think of them as part of current income rather than a one-time windfall gain. As people become accustomed to the regular payments, there is also the worry that this will undermine incentives to work.

To sum up, even though multiple payments could give a bigger boost to consumption during a recession, this must be balanced with microeconomic, implementation and other practical disadvantages.

Conclusions

Since the late 1990s, discretionary transfers have become a more important component of the Singapore government's social expenditures and an important tool for macroeconomic stabilisation. In recent years, the government has also become more explicit in adopting counter-cyclical fiscal policies which "lean against the wind". This new fiscal approach — which goes beyond the traditional emphasis on supporting growth over the medium term — is largely the result of increased macroeconomic volatility. Given Singapore's relative paucity of automatic stabilisers in public expenditure, the government has had to rely more on discretionary fiscal transfers to assist lower-income Singaporeans and provide a measure of counter-cyclical support.

The shift in Singapore's tax structure — from direct taxation (mainly income taxes) to a more balanced one in which indirect taxation (the GST in particular) contributes a larger share of government revenues — has provided another impetus for the use of discretionary fiscal transfers. Because such a change in the tax structure is regressive, the government has had to develop new ways to provide compensating benefits to Singaporeans who do not benefit from the income tax reductions but have to cope with a higher GST rate.

Singapore's experience suggests that the successful design of discretionary transfers requires policymakers to be cognisant of cognitive biases or behavioural tendencies such as the following:

- **Lack of self-control:** If the intent is to encourage savings for the future, fiscal policymakers should consider limiting the ability of beneficiaries to consume the discretionary transfers immediately.
- **Sense of entitlement:** If the transfers are not intended to be permanent, fiscal policymakers should try to avoid a high degree of predictability in the design and composition of the discretionary transfers.
- **Framing:** How a discretionary transfer is framed can be an important determinant of whether it is spent or saved; "bonuses" are more likely to be spent than "rebates" or "offsets".
- **Mental accounting:** Fiscal policymakers should assess the relative merits of providing multiple transfers against lump sum transfers based on whether or not the goal is to increase consumption in the short term.

References

Abeysinghe, Tilak and Keen Meng Choy (2007). *The Singapore Economy: An Econometric Perspective*. Routledge.

Ando, Albert and Franco Modigliani (1963). "The Life Cycle Hypothesis of Saving: Aggregate Implications and Tests." *American Economic Review*, Vol. 53, No. 1, pp. 55–84.

Auerbach, Alan (2002). "Is There a Role for Discretionary Fiscal Policy?" *NBER Working Paper Series*, No. 9306.

Barro, Robert (1974). "Are Government Bonds Net Wealth?" *Journal of Political Economy*, Vol. 82, No. 6, pp. 1095–1117.

Beaulier, Scott and Bryan Caplan (2007). "Behavioural Economics and Perverse Effects of the Welfare State." *KYKLOS*, Vol. 60, No. 4, pp. 485–507.

Blanchard, Olivier and Roberto Perotti (2002). "An Empirical Characterization of the Dynamic Effects of Changes in Government Spending and Taxes on Output." *The Quarterly Journal of Economics*, Vol. 117, No. 4, pp. 1329–1368.

Blinder, Alan (2006). "The Case Against the Case Against Discretionary Fiscal Policy," in Richard Kopcke, Geoffrey Tootell and Robert Triest, eds., *The Macroeconomics of Fiscal Policy*, pp. 25–61. MIT Press.

Burtless, Gary (2009). *Social Protection for the Economic Crisis: The US Experience*. The Brookings Institution.

Chambers, Valrie and Marilyn Spencer (2008). "Does Changing the Timing of a Yearly Individual Tax Refund Change the Amount Spent vs. Saved?" *Journal of Economic Psychology*, Vol. 29, No. 6, pp. 856–862.

Congressional Budget Office, United States Congress (2009). *Estimated Macroeconomic Effects of the American Recovery and Reinvestment Act of 2009*, Washington D.C.

Feldstein, Martin (2002). "The Role for Discretionary Fiscal Policy in a Low Interest Rate Environment." *NBER Working Paper 9203*, National Bureau of Economic Research.

Friedman, Milton (1953). "The Effects of a Full Employment Policy on Economic Stability: A Formal Analysis," in *Essays in Positive Economics*, pp. 117–132. Chicago University Press.

Friedman, Milton (1957). *A Theory of the Consumption Function*. Princeton University Press.

Hu, Richard (1992). "Budget Statement 1992", viewed 10 August 2009, http://www.parliament.gov.sg/reports/private/hansard/full/19920228/19920228_HR.htm

Keeler, James, William James and Mohamed Abdel-Ghany (1985). "The Relative Size of Windfall Income and the Permanent Income Hypothesis." *Journal of Business and Economic Statistics*, Vol. 3, No. 3, pp. 209–215.

Landsberger, Michael (1966). "Windfall Income and Consumption: Comment." *American Economic Review*, Vol. 56, No. 3, pp. 534–540.

Lee, Hsien Loong (2003). *Interview by David Skilling of Harvard University's Kennedy School of Government*, video recording, Civil Service College, Singapore.

Lucas, Robert Jr. (1976). "Econometric Policy Evaluation: a Critique," in Karl Brunner and Allan Meltzer, eds., *The Phillips Curve and Labor Markets*, *Carnegie-Rochester Conference Series on Public Policy*, Vol. 1, pp. 19–46.

OECD (2009). "The Effectiveness and Scope of Fiscal Stimulus", *OECD Economic Outlook: Interim Report, March 2009*, viewed 20 January 2011, http://www.oecd.org/dataoecd/3/62/42421337.pdf

Perotti, Roberto (2002). "Estimating the Effects of Fiscal Policy in OECD Countries." *European Central Bank Working Paper* 168.

Shapiro, Matthew and Joel Slemrod (2003a). "Consumer Response to Tax Rebates." *American Economic Review*, Vol. 93, No. 1, pp. 381–396.

Shapiro, Matthew and Joel Slemrod (2003b). "Did the 2001 Tax Rebate Stimulate Spending? Evidence from Taxpayer Surveys." *Tax Policy and the Economy*, Vol. 17, pp. 83–109.

Thaler, Richard (1992). *The Winner's Curse: Paradoxes and Anomalies of Economic Life*. Princeton University Press.

Thaler, Richard (1999). "Mental Accounting Matters." *Journal of Behavioural Decision Making*, Vol. 12, No. 3, pp. 183–206.

Thaler, Richard and Cass Sunstein (2008). *Nudge: Improving Decisions about Health, Wealth and Happiness*. Yale University Press.

Tversky, Amos and Daniel Kahneman (1974). "Judgment Under Uncertainty: Heuristics and Biases." *Science*, Vol. 185, No. 4157, pp. 1124–1131.

Van den Noord, Paul (2000). "The Size and Role of Automatic Fiscal Stabilisers in the 1990s and Beyond." *Working Paper* 230, OECD Economics Department.

Appendix: Discretionary Fiscal Transfers, 1992–2009

Discretionary Fiscal Transfer	Year/s Given
REBATES	
Service and Conservancy Charges (S&CC) Rebates	
S&CC rebates were given to Singaporean households living in public housing, to offset the monthly maintenance charges collected by town councils. Households in smaller-sized flats received larger rebates.	1992, 2005–2010
Rental Rebates	
Rental rebates were given to Singaporeans who live in rented public housing, to help offset their rental costs.	1993, 2005–2010
Utilities Rebates (U-Save)	
U-Save rebates were given to Singaporeans living in public housing to offset their utility charges. Households in smaller-sized flats received larger U-Save rebates.	1997–2001, 2004–2010
TOP-UPS TO SAVINGS	
Central Provident Fund (CPF) Top-Ups	
The CPF is a fully-funded, defined contribution, social security system based on individual savings accounts. Participation in the CPF is mandatory for employed Singaporeans and permanent residents. CPF contributions are credited into three accounts: (i) the Ordinary Account, which can be used for property, higher education and approved investments; (ii) the Medisave Account, which can be used to pay for hospitalization expenses, certain types of outpatient care and approved medical insurance; and (iii) the Special Account, which is designated only for retirement purposes, it can only be used for investment in retirement-related financial products.	
Top-Ups to the CPF-Ordinary Account and/or Special Account	
The government topped up the CPF accounts of Singaporeans seven times from 1993 to 2006. For example, in 2001, Singaporeansreceived CPF top-ups of S$500 to S$1,700 as part of a surplus-sharing initiative, at a total cost of S$1 billion to the government. More recently in 2006, Singaporeans aged 50 and above each received CPF top-ups of S$100 in their Special Accounts at a cost of S$80 million.	1993, 1995, 1996, 2000, 2001, 2005, 2006

(Continued)

(Continued)

Discretionary Fiscal Transfer	Year/s Given
Top-Ups to Medisave Account The government topped up the Medisave Accounts of Singaporeans seven times between 1996 and 2010. For example,in 2008, Singaporeans aged 51 and above each received top-ups of up to S$550 (older Singaporeans received more), costing a a total of S$226 million.	1996, 1997, 2004–2006, 2008, 2010
Top-Ups to Post- Secondary Education Account (PSEA) The PSEA scheme was introduced in 2007 to help Singaporeans with post-secondary education expenses. The PSEA provides government co-funding for parents who save for the post-secondary needs of their children. The money can be used for approved fees and charges at post-secondary educational institutions. The government has topped up PSEAs three times since 2007. For example, in 2008, Singaporeans aged 7 to 20 each received PSEA top-ups of up to S$1,000, at a total cost of S$500 million.	2007, 2008, 2010

SHARES

New Singapore Shares (NSS) The NSS were introduced in 2001 to help Singaporeans cope with the economic downturn at the time. Depending on income, Singaporeans received between S$200 and S$1,700 of NSS, with lower-income citizens receiving more. The NSS earned annual dividends, in the form of bonus shares, over 5 years. The bonus shares were guaranteed at a minimum rate of 3%, plus the real GDP growth rate (if positive) of the preceding calendar year. Singaporeans could also exchange their allotted NSS for cash, although not all at once (up to 50% within the first year). The NSS cost S$2.5 billion.	2001–2002

(Continued)

(Continued)

Discretionary Fiscal Transfer	Year/s Given
Economic Restructuring Shares (ERS)	2003–2005

The ERS were part of a larger offset package to help Singaporeans adjust to the structural changes in the economy, especially the increase in the Goods and Services Tax (GST) rate from 3% to 5% in 2003 to 2005. The ERS were given out in three allotments, with one lot each year starting from 2003. Depending on their housing type, Singaporeans received between S$600 and S$1,200 of ERS. Like the NSS, the ERS earned annual dividends, in the form of bonus shares, over 5 years. The bonus shares were guaranteed at a minimum rate of 3%, plus the real GDP growth rate (if positive) of the preceding calendar year. Singaporeans could exchange their ERS into cash and they could also do so immediately, at any time. The ERS cost the government S$2.7 billion.

CASH TRANSFERS

Progress Package: Growth Dividends and NS Bonus

The 2006 Growth Dividends (S$1.4 billion) and 40th Anniversary NS Bonus (S$200 million) were direct cash transfers given to all adult Singaporeans. All adult Singaporeans received between S$200 and S$800 of Growth Dividends, with lower-income citizens receiving more. Those who had served National Service (compulsory military service for Singapore males) received the 40th Anniversary NS Bonus of S$400. Singaporeans received these cash transfers between 1 May 2006 and 31 December 2006. *(2006, 2008)*

The Growth Dividends were again given in the 2008 Budget. Later that year, the government increased the amount of 2008 Growth Dividends that Singaporeans received, to help them cope with rising costs. Including the enhancement, adult Singaporeans received between S$125 and S$850 in 2008, with older Singaporeans and those on lower incomes receiving more. Singaporeans received these cash transfers in two instalments between 1 April 2008 and 31 December 2008. The 2008 package cost the government S$1.06 billion.

(Continued)

(Continued)

Discretionary Fiscal Transfer	Year/s Given
GST Offset Package: GST Credits and Senior Citizens' Bonus The GST Credits (S$1.8 billion) and Senior Citizens' Bonus (S$400 million) were introduced as direct cash transfers for all Singaporeans, to help them adjust to the increase in GST from 5% to 7% in 2007. The GST Credits were given annually over four years, starting from 1 July 2007. All adult Singaporeans received between S$100 and S$2,000 of GST Credits and Senior Citizens' Bonus, with older Singaporeans and those on lower incomes receiving more.	2007–2010
The Government doubled the amount of GST Credits and Senior Citizens' Bonus that Singaporeans received in 2009, to help them cope with the economic crisis. Singaporeans received this additional payout on 1 March 2009, at an additional cost to government of S$580 million.	

CHAPTER 7

USING BEHAVIOURAL INSIGHTS TO IMPROVE INDIVIDUAL HEALTH DECISIONS

Lavinia LOW and YEE Yiling

> "...surely we are capable of behaviour change when our own welfare is at stake, yes? Sadly, no. If we were, every diet would always work (and there would be no need for diets in the first place). If we were, most smokers would be ex-smokers... ...But knowing and doing are two different things, especially when pleasure is involved."

Levitt and Dubner (2009)

Introduction

Over the last thirty years, public healthcare reforms in Singapore have centred on sharpening incentives for citizens to take care of their own health; on financing healthcare more efficiently (for example, through compulsory savings for healthcare and a national insurance scheme); on targeting subsidies at those who need them most; and on promoting healthy lifestyle choices. To a significant extent, these reforms have been shaped and influenced by economics and its analysis of market failures in healthcare. Conventional economics provided, and continues to provide, useful guidance to health policies in Singapore.

But good policymaking in public healthcare requires more than a faithful adherence to the economist's adage of ensuring the right incentives. Incentives, while important, are sometimes an insufficient guide for policy formulation in public healthcare and an incomplete explanation of people's decisions and behaviours in healthcare.

The standard economic assumption of rational agency often does not apply to healthcare. For example, we all know that regular exercise is good for us, yet how many of us hit the gym regularly or choose the stairs over the lift? Why is it uncommon for individuals to have healthy diets? Rationality assumes that we calculate the probabilities and associated costs of healthcare and save or insure accordingly. But do we really apply such rigorous cost-benefit analyses in deciding how much to save or insure for healthcare?

Behavioural economics tells us that people have the most difficulty making good choices when their decisions involve risk and uncertainty or require them to sacrifice current benefits for future gain. These characteristics are common in many health decisions, such as how much one should save or insure for medical contingencies and whether and when to consume healthcare (Liebman and Zeckhauser 2008).

In this chapter, we first provide an overview of the standard economic explanations for why healthcare markets — left on their own — do not always work well. These explanations provide a large part of the rationale for the Singapore government's interventions in healthcare. We then examine the perspectives offered by behavioural economics on why the rational choice model is not always a good approximation of how people make health decisions. Applying these insights to Singapore, we discuss how behavioural economics can improve healthcare policies and help individuals make better health decisions.

Market Failures in Healthcare: The Usual Suspects

Markets work best when the following assumptions hold true: competitive markets, low barriers of entry for new producers, easy availability of information, symmetry of information between sellers and buyers, and product homogeneity. In healthcare, however, many of these assumptions are not very realistic.

The Consumption of Healthcare

Healthcare is not a "normal" good like a meal or a mobile phone. For most goods, lower consumption equates to a lower quality of life. This is not always the case in healthcare. For people with a serious medical condition, healthcare is a necessity: reducing consumption could mean death, not just a poorer quality of life. Conversely, there are also healthcare services or products which are not necessary. Take for instance the availability of expensive designer drugs and generic drugs in the market, both of which are equally effective. The consumer who purchases the more expensive drug does not necessarily enjoy a higher quality of life even though he has spent more.

In healthcare, the distribution of information is often uneven. Consider the relationship between the provider (in this case, doctor) and the consumer (the patient). Markets work well when both parties have (more or less) equal access to information. In healthcare, patients generally do not know enough about medicine and rely heavily on the advice of their doctors. This gives the provider the power to create a higher demand for healthcare services than necessary, a problem known as "supplier-induced demand". Left to its own devices, an unregulated healthcare market may well result in higher consumption of healthcare than is necessary or socially desirable.

Another peculiar feature of the healthcare market is that the patient is often not the direct payer for the services consumed. Instead, the payer is often a third party: either the government (if tax revenues finance a significant share of healthcare costs) or a private insurance company (if the patient is covered by health insurance). That the individual consumer is not the payer produces some unusual consequences, as we shall soon see.

The amount of money spent on healthcare over one's lifetime also varies significantly from person to person. Not everyone will meet with catastrophic illnesses. Rather than requiring everyone to save substantial amounts for all medical contingencies, using insurance as a financing tool for catastrophic illnesses is more efficient. Under an insurance scheme, each member of the insured population contributes a small sum to a pooled fund which is used to help the small proportion of the population that incurs large medical bills. Health insurance allows us to enjoy protection against the risks of large bills without any of us having to save fully for them.

However, private insurance suffers from informational asymmetries as well. Individuals know more about their health status and conditions than the insurance companies that are paying the bills. People who know they are at a higher risk of requiring expensive healthcare will want more insurance and are willing to pay more. Those who have better health will be less willing to pay for medical insurance. Therefore, for any level of premium, the insurer will attract only the people who consider the premium "cheap". This means that the insurer ends up with the bad risks — a problem known as adverse selection. It leaves the insurer in a bind: if he increases premiums to cover his (now higher) costs, he will simply attract those with even higher healthcare risks and cause those with lower risks to drop out — leaving him with an even poorer risk pool.

Knowing this, health insurance companies will try to avoid adverse selection by "cherry picking", or restricting their coverage only to the good risks, such as the young and those with no pre-existing medical conditions. This suggests that when left to market forces, private health insurance is unlikely to provide adequate coverage and will exclude those who need it the most. Relying only on private insurance will therefore result in unequal access to good healthcare.

The failure of private health insurance markets to provide for universal coverage makes it tempting for governments to socialise healthcare entirely and finance it through general taxation or through social insurance in which there is universal participation. While this solves the cherry picking problem, it does not eliminate the problem of moral hazard and may even compound it. When consumers enjoy free or heavily subsidised healthcare, they have less incentive to be prudent in their consumption decisions. The outcome could be over-consumption and a less-than-efficient allocation of resources to healthcare.

The Production of Healthcare

Besides the market failures in the consumption of healthcare, there are also certain aspects of healthcare production that make it less than efficient. For instance, it takes years to train medical professionals — doctors, surgeons, nurses or allied health professionals. The high cost of training — both time and opportunity costs — creates barriers of entry to those who wish to enter the healthcare profession. In addition, certain specialities require skills that are not easily acquired. An example would be neurosurgery where dexterous hands and the ability to work long hours under highly stressful conditions are required over and above medical knowledge. These represent high sunk costs and barriers to entry for producers. Without some form of government intervention — say in the form of subsidies for expensive medical training — these barriers could result in a shortage of medical services and high costs in specialist care. Access to good healthcare by lower-income citizens could also be compromised.

Healthcare Through the Lens of Behavioural Economics

Behavioural economics provides additional arguments for why the healthcare market does not function as efficiently as most other markets. First, people do not usually consider the risk or probability that they might require expensive medical care because they do not want to think about bad outcomes. Liebman and Zeckhauser (2008) argue that even if we wanted to contemplate medical risks and probabilities, we often lack the computational capacity or the relevant information to do so. Similarly, Kahneman *et al.* (1986) posit that naïve accounting leads us to make systematic mistakes when assessing probabilities.

Secondly, medical expenditures tend to be highly lumpy and uncertain. This suggests that individuals should pool their risks and obtain health insurance. But the health insurance decision is more complex than with, say, homeowners' or life insurance because there are so many possible "loss events", including many which are unfamiliar to the consumer (Liebman and Zeckhauser 2008). Consequently, it is not realistic to assume that people would purchase health insurance using a rational, cost-benefit calculus. It is more likely that people choose from among a limited range of insurance policies that are put before them.

Thirdly, people often rely on rules of thumb to make their healthcare decisions. For instance, they may observe the experiences and behaviours of their friends, relatives and co-workers in order to make their own healthcare decisions, or they may draw conclusions about the risks of particular illnesses based on their experiences or those of celebrities. This is known as availability bias. But such rules of thumb are not always reliable. The low-probability, high-impact nature of many healthcare episodes exacerbates the inadequacy of relying only on one's observations and experiences. We are also more likely to pay attention to well-publicised but low-probability ailments than to high-probability but less well-known conditions (such as coronary diseases and obesity).

Fourth, many healthcare decisions require individuals to forgo some short-term benefits for longer-term gains. Much like saving for retirement, health worries are often not immediate and are therefore easy to delay. In this context, health insurance and savings — which require some short-term loss to deal with a future contingency — are usually not salient in the minds of most people, and they are therefore often put off.

Many other decisions in healthcare also require some sacrifice in the near term for a future benefit: the decision to eat more healthily, to quit smoking, to exercise regularly, to invest in preventive care now, or to take measures to prevent a chronic illness from worsening. One of the main insights of behavioural economics is that when faced with such decisions, individuals tend to place excessive weight on current costs and under-weight future benefits, a tendency known as present-biased preferences (Loewenstein *et al.* 2007).

Individuals also tend to apply a huge discount factor between today and the future even though their discount rate between two future events is usually low. This pattern of applying inconsistent discount rates is called hyperbolic discounting, and it leads to procrastination and inertia — the habit of putting something unpleasant off for another day.

Healthcare Financing in Singapore

In light of all the "failures" discussed above, it is not surprising that healthcare is an area where a significant degree of government regulation, subsidy and provision is widely considered necessary.

The Singapore government's approach to healthcare has been to intervene in ways that are commensurate with the extent of market failure and in areas where the informational asymmetries are most severe. Some segments of the healthcare sector are more prone to market failures than others. For instance, it is easier for consumers to obtain reliable information on common ailments that can be treated in a primary care setting than on medical conditions requiring specialist treatment or acute care. Consequently, the government is more involved in the acute care sector than in primary care. The vast majority of hospital beds are provided by the public sector, while private general practitioners play a larger role in the primary care setting.

The government's approach is also to vary healthcare financing according to how much individuals can be expected to bear part of the financial risks of falling ill. For instance in primary care, patients are expected to bear a larger share because the costs are relatively low, and self-financing encourages them to look after their own health. With catastrophic illnesses, it would not be efficient or equitable to expect patients to bear most of the costs because they are much higher. For such low-probability and high-impact episodes, some form of risk pooling — whether through private or social insurance — is a better financing arrangement.

Ensuring the right balance between individual responsibility and social protection has been the central preoccupation of healthcare financing in Singapore over the years. Today's system is a hybrid of public and private funding, with multiple tiers of protection to ensure affordable healthcare.

The first tier consists of significant government funding to tertiary care institutions (such as hospitals) and other intermediate and long-term care institutions. The second tier comprises individual savings that can be used to meet hospitalisation expenses and costly outpatient treatments. Working Singaporeans and permanent residents are required to save a percentage of their incomes through Medisave, which is a part of the Central Provident Fund (CPF), Singapore's primary social security system. The third tier consists of risk pooling through a low-cost health insurance scheme for catastrophic illness (MediShield) and a long-term care insurance scheme for severe disability (ElderShield). Finally, a social safety net exists in the form of Medifund, a government-funded endowment that provides assistance for those with no other means of financial support.

Medisave

Behavioural economics suggests that due to individuals' inconsistent discount rates over different time horizons, we generally prefer to consume today and defer savings to tomorrow. But when tomorrow becomes today, we often defer the decision again. We tend to pay more attention to present utility and ignore or heavily discount the long-term benefits of forgoing current consumption. Medisave pre-empts such procrastination by enforcing medical savings among working Singaporeans and permanent residents.

Medisave was started in 1984 to help Singaporeans take responsibility for their own healthcare needs. Although not strictly guided by behavioural economics, the government of the day grasped its essential insight that people, left on their own, were unlikely to cater for a future benefit (i.e. being able to afford healthcare services) by incurring a smaller cost in the present (i.e. saving).

As with a social insurance scheme, employees set aside a certain percentage of their income: 7% to 9.5% of an employee's monthly income (up to S$5,000) is channelled into Medisave. But unlike social insurance, this contribution is placed in the individual's medical savings account for his or his immediate family's hospital-isation needs and costly outpatient treatments.

Medisave has proved to be a reliable financing tool for acute care expenses; eight out of ten Singaporeans use Medisave for their inpatient stays. At the same time, withdrawal limits are put in place to ensure that savings are conserved for future medical needs, especially during old age, and are not depleted in a single episode. This again reflects the objective — consistent with behavioural economics — of helping people meet today's needs without compromising their ability to meet future needs.

But why rely on individual savings in addition to insurance? Part of the answer lies in the government's concerns over moral hazard: people are more likely to be careful when spending their own money. Medisave thus encourages citizens to consume healthcare services more carefully as a savings rather than an insurance scheme.

MediShield, ElderShield and Integrated Shield Plans

While Medisave helps to finance the hospitalisation expenses for most Singaporeans, relying on savings alone would not suffice for low probability, high cost medical episodes. Thus, MediShield was introduced in 1990 as a basic catastrophic illness insurance scheme. Part of an employee's Medisave contributions is channelled into MediShield. Later, Medisave-approved but privately-provided insurance plans were introduced for those who wanted greater coverage.

When MediShield was introduced, the Singapore government sought to ensure that as many people as possible were covered. Standard economic theory offers little guidance on how a government should go about maximising the insurance coverage of a population. According to rational choice models, consumers would purchase the optimal amount of insurance on their own accord: as long as the marginal benefit of obtaining more insurance outweighed its marginal cost, consumers would increase their coverage. In practice however, it is unlikely that individuals engage in such cost-benefit calculations, or are even able to do so.

Two features of MediShield deserve particular mention. First, MediShield is run on an opt-out basis. Since the scheme began, working adults have been automatically included in MediShield through their (mandatory) participation in Medisave.[1] In 2007, measures were put in place to automatically cover newborn Singaporeans and permanent residents. Significant efforts have also gone into reaching out to school-going children through auto-cover exercises administered by schools. Together, these efforts have raised the overall coverage of MediShield[2] to 88% of Singapore's resident population, a large improvement over the coverage of 51% in 1990. ElderShield, a basic severe disability insurance scheme which started in 2002, works in a similar way with auto-coverage for working Singaporeans when they turn 40.

Behavioural economics explains the high coverage levels of MediShield and ElderShield using the concept of status quo bias or endowment effect. This refers to the tendency of individuals to leave things as they are and not to switch out of the default position set for them by the authorities. As predicted by behavioural economics, the national insurance schemes of MediShield and ElderShield — by setting participation as the default position — have achieved very high participation rates.

At the same time, the government did not want all Singaporeans to be solely reliant on the default option of MediShield. After all, it is meant to provide only basic coverage. Singaporeans who wanted higher coverage and could afford higher premiums were encouraged to take up more insurance. In the earlier years when

---

[1] This was achieved by enrolling workers into MediShield upon their first contribution into their CPF accounts.
[2] As of end 2010 and inclusive of Integrated Shield Plans.

Medisave-approved private plans were introduced, acquiring higher coverage meant exiting the MediShield subscriber pool and joining the private insurer's risk pool. However, cherry picking by insurers resulted in the risk profile of MediShield subscribers deteriorating over time. To address this problem, the entire industry of Medisave-approved private plans was restructured. Today, any health insurance plan that can be paid from Medisave must be "integrated" with MediShield as the foundation block. This has kept the MediShield risk pool intact, while still providing individuals with the option of obtaining higher coverage. 58% of the MediShield-insured population are now covered by these Integrated Plans.

In addition to the opt-out mechanism, the other key feature of MediShield and the Integrated Plans is that the premiums are payable from individuals' Medisave accounts. This reduces the out-of-pocket costs of health insurance. From a behavioural perspective, this helps to circumvent the problem of loss aversion — the tendency of people to value losses more than gains — that would occur if people were required to make out-of-pocket contributions.

Helping Citizens Make Better Health Choices

Other than the health financing regime, health policymakers in Singapore have also sought ways to help citizens make better health-related decisions in health and to keep healthcare in Singapore affordable. Behavioural insights help to shed light on some of the policy problems commonly faced by health policymakers.

Use of Generics as Default

The branding of drugs, just as with other consumer goods, is a means for pharmaceutical companies to distinguish their products from others. However, once a drug is off-patent, rival pharmaceutical companies can manufacture generic drugs with the same active ingredients and therefore achieve the same efficacy as the incumbent, branded drug. (Indeed, some pharmaceutical companies have responded to the challenge of generic manufacturers and now have a generic arm with the intent of cornering both segments of the market.) In a normal market, we assume consumers know this and make decisions on the basis of price only.

In the healthcare market however, doctors are the ones who prescribe drugs. If the market was left unchecked, aggressive marketing by pharmaceutical companies could enhance incentives for doctors to prescribe the branded and more expensive drugs even if cheaper, generic alternatives are available. To avoid this outcome, Singapore's restructured hospitals are required to prescribe generic drugs as the default. This helps to keep healthcare costs down. Non-generics would be considered as second-line treatment, for example in the event that the patient does not react well to the generic drug, or if the patient prefers branded drugs (with higher patient co-payment to limit over-servicing and to discourage over-consumption).

Anti-Smoking Measures

Habits play a significant role in our everyday lives. Behavioural economics offers some plausible explanations for why people choose to smoke despite being aware of its harmful effects. Because of present-biased preferences and hyperbolic discounting, people tend to focus on the immediate satisfaction that smoking brings and under-estimate its future cost to their health, especially since smoking-related illnesses such as lung cancer and chronic obstructive pulmonary disease (COPD) are delayed and occur only many years later. This lack of saliency — combined with smokers' over-confidence and excessive optimism — is likely to be a major contributing factor to the persistence of the smoking habit. Smokers may also view others suffering from smoking-related diseases as the unlucky "X%". Put another way, individuals tend to think "it will happen to someone else, not me".

The main policy tool to discourage smoking provided by standard neoclassical economics is the use of taxation to force smokers to internalise the social cost of their actions. However, since conventional economics does not explain why individuals engage in self-harming behaviours in the first place, this policy solution is not entirely satisfactory. In addition to imposing hefty tobacco duties, the Singapore government has pursued additional measures aimed at changing social norms and making smoking as inconvenient as possible. These measures include designating all indoor spaces as smoke-free zones, limiting spaces designated for smoking, and requiring that tobacco companies carry warning messages related to smoking, along with graphic images of rotten gums and blackened lungs on cigarette packs.

In behavioural terms, making smoking inconvenient in public places discourages smoking by exploiting the very same trait that contributes to the smoking habit: the present-biased preferences that lead individuals to place a disproportionate weight on their immediate utility. The measure works by increasing the immediate cost —— in this case time and effort —— for a smoker to light up, thereby making the choice of not smoking a (marginally) more convenient and less costly one.

Altering individuals' perceptions of benefits and costs and influencing social norms are probably more effective in discouraging people from picking up smoking than it is in encouraging current smokers to quit. Old habits die hard. Behavioural economics suggests other ways in which governments can work with people's present-biased preferences. For example, a smoker is often more willing to deny him or herself tomorrow's cigarettes than today's. Governments might consider taking advantage of this by getting smokers to participate in programmes which stipulate a reduction and final abstinence from smoking and which impose financial penalties if they fail to meet the goal. The financial penalty increases the saliency of the loss from reneging on the individual's commitment to quit. Studies on drug addicts have found that addicts tend to place more weight on immediate, tangible benefits than on less tangible, distant gains (Loewenstein *et al.* 2007).

Influencing Food Choices and Combating Obesity

In a similar vein, individuals with weight management or health problems are less inclined to adhere to their recommended diet regimes as the benefits of becoming healthier are delayed and less tangible than the immediate gratification from having their favourite food. The Health Promotion Board (HPB) in Singapore has sought to influence dietary behaviours by providing healthier options to common foods instead of advocating complete avoidance of unhealthy foods. To aid consumers, food outlets which use healthier ingredients can be easily identified by the "Healthier Choice" logos that are displayed at their stalls.

Behavioural economists support such actions as they attempt to exploit people's present-biased preferences by altering their short-term incentives (making healthier food more convenient and less "costly" to their immediate well-being) rather than to get individuals to make decisions based on their long-term interests. Constantly reminding individuals about the healthier choices available to them aims to nudge and shape their behaviours in desired directions.

Increasing Organ Donations Through Defaults

As Eric Johnson and Dan Goldstein have found in their online experiment on people's willingness to be organ donors under different default options, the choice of defaults makes a huge difference to participation levels in organ donation programmes (Goldstein and Johnson 2003). In the experiment, survey participants were presented with one of three options on organ donation: (i) opt-in, with non-participation as the default option; (ii) opt-out with participation as the default option; and (iii) a neutral option where participants had to choose either to be an organ donor or a non-organ donor with no prior default. To eliminate inconvenience costs (e.g. filling up of forms, going for a medical test), all that was needed was a mouse-click to either confirm their choice to remain with the default option or to change their status. The results: 42% chose to be an organ donor under the opt-in scenario; 82% remained as donors under the opt-out scheme and 79% indicated their intention to be a donor under the neutral option. This experiment suggests that although most people wish to be a donor (as shown by the neutral scenario), many do not choose to do so even if the effort required is minimal.

Data collected by Johnson and Goldstein from various European countries also show a higher effective consent rate[3] for opt-out schemes than for opt-in schemes. This in turn translates to a higher number of organ transplant procedures.

In organ donations, behavioural economics seems to be a better predictor than conventional economic models which predict that people would choose the same option as long as the relative pay-offs are the same. In Singapore's context, the Human Organ Transplant Act (HOTA) sets participation in organ donation as the default unless individuals opt-out. This has helped raise our organ transplant rates. Subsequent revisions to the legislation[4] now allow for the donation of the kidney, liver, heart and cornea in the event of death and covers all Singaporeans aged 21 and above who are of sound mind, unless they opt-out.

---

[3] Effective donor rate is taken as the number of people who had opted in (in explicit-consent countries) or the number who had not opted out (in presumed consent countries).

[4] As of 1 November 2009, the upper age limit of 60 years was removed, increasing the pool of effective donors.

Cadaveric organ transplant numbers have since climbed. For example, kidney donation by deceased donors averaged around five per year before the enactment of HOTA in 1987. This number rose to an average of 49 per year during the period between 2004 and June 2007. With each deceased donor potentially donating multiple organs, many more patients have benefited.

Communicating Difficult Policy Decisions

From time to time, health policymakers in Singapore have found it necessary not only to design and implement unpopular policy decisions, but also to communicate and explain them to a sceptical public. In this section, we look at a recent example of how the Singapore government communicated its decision to introduce means testing in publicly subsidised hospitals.

Means testing is the practice of differentiating the levels of healthcare subsidy a patient receives based on his or her level of income. It is a more efficient approach than broad-based or universal subsidies because it targets subsidies at those who need it the most. It therefore reduces the overall cost of healthcare to taxpayers.

Means testing for inpatient hospitalisation had been considered by the Singapore government as far back as the early 1980s as a way of preventing well-off patients from crowding out lower-income patients from highly subsidised hospital beds. Although frequently considered, it was only in the early years of the 21st century that the government took serious steps to introduce means testing in public hospitals.

Getting the public to accept means testing was (and continues to be) a major communications challenge as some would be entitled to a lower subsidy level and therefore have to pay higher prices. A successful policy communications effort thus requires an understanding of people's perceptions of equity and fairness.

Singapore's Ministry of Health (MOH) invested much effort in engaging and persuading the public before rolling out means testing. Extensive public consultation was carried out in 2008 to understand the public's response, explain the larger societal benefits and impacts, and to clarify misconceptions. Means testing was also designed to be implemented with 16 graduated bands of 1% each, so that the reduction of subsidies for those caught at the margins would be small. To minimise administrative hassle for patients and their families, information on their income bands would be automatically obtained by the hospitals.

Communications on means testing was also kept concise. The essential message conveyed was that means testing was necessary to allocate limited resources to those who need it most. At the same time, those with special circumstances would be considered for additional assistance. It was also emphasised that means testing would not restrict the patient's choice of ward class. This meant that even if the subsidies (to which they were entitled) were reduced as a result of means testing, higher-income patients could still choose the cheaper ward classes.

The design and eventual implementation of means testing took into account the major concerns of the public, including their perception of fairness — another area of study in behavioural economics. Kahneman *et al.* (1986) conducted telephone surveys to find out people's perception of fairness of price hikes under different circumstances. The findings revealed that the majority of respondents considered it acceptable for prices to be raised in response to cost increases, but not if the price hike was the result of an increase in demand or market power. It also indicated that most would agree to allow capital owners (employers, landlords and merchants) to maintain a positive buffer between revenue and cost and that it would not be unreasonable for them to pass on higher costs to the consumer, if the price increases were due to a rise in the cost of inputs.

In a similar vein, it is equitable to expect patients with more "financial means" to take on a larger share of the burden of rising healthcare costs. Means testing was presented as a way of allocating scarce resources in healthcare in a fairer, more equitable way. Communicating the purpose of means testing along these lines may have been one of the factors that led to public acceptance of the policy.

Conclusion

In the last three decades, health policymakers in Singapore have sought to put in place the right incentives for citizens to economise and exercise prudence in their healthcare consumption decisions and to take care of their own health. Conventional economics has provided useful guidance to that end. At the same time, healthcare policymakers have been aware that people do not always act in ways that conform to standard economics. Cognitive biases, particularly the human tendency to heavily discount the future and to procrastinate, have a major influence on people's health decisions and behaviours. The combination of ensuring the right incentives and taking into account behavioural realities has contributed to an efficient healthcare system. Although Singapore spends less than 4% of GDP in healthcare, its health outcomes are comparable to (and often surpass) other developed countries which spend much more on healthcare.

Singapore's relatively low level of spending in healthcare is also partly the result of a relatively youthful population. With its population ageing rapidly, the government will have to rethink and adapt many of its healthcare policies. It will have to fine-tune the balance between savings and insurance, encourage Singaporeans to make better health decisions (healthier lifestyles, better diets), further develop long-term care insurance, strengthen the delivery of long-term care, and improve the management of chronic diseases. In these and other health policy challenges, behavioural economics may suggest interesting and potentially transformative ways of improving health outcomes.

References

Goldstein, Daniel and Eric Johnson (2003). "Do Defaults Save Lives?" *Science*, Vol. 302, No. 5649, pp. 1338–1339.

Kahneman, Daniel, Jack Knetsch and Richard Thaler (1986). "Fairness as a Constraint on Profit Seeking: Entitlement in the Market." *The American Economic Review*, Vol. 76, No. 4, pp. 728–741.

Levitt, Steven and Stephen Dubner (2009). *SuperFreakonomics: Global Cooling, Patriotic Prostitutes, and Why Suicide Bombers Should Buy Life Insurance*. William Morrow.

Liebman, Jeffrey and Richard Zeckhauser (2008). "Simple Humans, Complex Insurance and Subtle Subsidies." *NBER Working Paper*, No. 14330, National Bureau of Economic Research.

Loewenstein, George, Troyen Brennan and Kevin Volpp (2007). "Asymmetric Paternalism to Improve Health Behaviors." *Journal of the American Medical Association*, Vol. 298, No. 20, pp. 2415–2417.

CHAPTER 8

A BEHAVIOURAL VIEW ON DESIGNING SINGAPORE'S NATIONAL ANNUITY SCHEME

Donald LOW[1]

> "People have a hard time knowing what to save. They have a hard time envisioning themselves in a distant future and envisioning how much they will or will not need to consume."
>
> Akerlof and Shiller (2009)

> "... the seemingly haphazard nature of saving, the failure to save, the sensitivity of saving to framing — are remarkable for their deviation from what economists currently say about the saving decision."
>
> Akerlof and Shiller (2009)

Introduction

Many governments in the developed world are grappling with how to reform and redesign their social security systems. As one of the world's fastest ageing nations, Singapore is no different. Singapore inherited a system of compulsory employee savings called the Central Provident Fund (CPF) from its British colonial days. The CPF has been the cornerstone of Singapore's social

[1] The author wishes to thank Don Yeo, Deputy Chief Executive Officer (Policy & Corporate Development Group) of the CPF Board, for the in-depth interviews and Chen Yanying, also of the CPF Board, for the excellent research support. The opinions expressed in this chapter represent the views of the author and should not be attributed to the CPF Board.

security system ever since. But the country's demographics were gradually rendering the CPF system inadequate to the task. Beyond individual savings, more was needed to provide financial security for a citizen's latter years.

Yet redesigning social security for an ageing population would prove to be a complicated undertaking. With a base of over 3 million members, any change to the CPF system would have to be broadly persuasive and flexible enough to meet a wide range of needs and aspirations.

This chapter describes the design and introduction of a national life annuity scheme, a major part of Singapore's social security reforms in recent years. Citizen concerns and responses to the scheme were wide-ranging and not wholly anticipated, and the shape of the annuity scheme evolved along the way. This chapter will explore how behavioural economics can help policymakers understand and address citizens' needs, while still meeting their policy objectives.

The Need for a National Annuity Scheme

The CPF was set up to provide a measure of financial security to employees after their retirement. It is a pension fund comprising individual accounts to which employees and their employers make mandatory contributions.

Compared with the social security systems commonly found in developed countries, the CPF system has three unique advantages. The first is that it is a fully-funded system and not one financed on a "pay-as-you-go" basis in which the retirement needs of today's workers are supported by future generations of workers. Being a fully-funded system means that an ageing population will not create unfunded liabilities for the state in terms of future pension provisions. Second, the CPF encourages individual responsibility and strengthens work incentives as one's retirement savings depend on his or her participation in work. Third, by mandating individual savings, the CPF gets around the problem commonly encountered in savings — people's procrastination and inertia in giving up current consumption for future (higher) consumption.

The CPF system was established in 1955, when Singapore's population was relatively youthful. The parameters were therefore appropriate for their time. But Singapore's demographic profile has been changing rapidly. In 1960, the average life expectancy was just 63 years; by 2006, it had risen to 80 years. Half of all Singaporeans aged 65 in 2006 are expected to live beyond age 85 (Department of Statistics, Singapore 2008). Yet CPF savings as a source of retirement income are designed to run out by about age 85. This is because under the original withdrawal policy,[2] CPF members would begin drawing on their funds from the drawdown age of 65[3] over a period of about 20 years. There was therefore a real need for Singapore's social security policymakers to rethink the CPF system and to address how it would meet the financial needs of citizens who live beyond 85.

What were the policy options available? An obvious one was to increase the CPF contribution rate. But there is broad agreement that the savings rate in Singapore is already very high, and that raising the employee's CPF contribution rates would reduce his disposable income for current consumption in favour of future needs that are more uncertain. Meanwhile, raising the employer's share of contributions to the CPF would raise business costs at a time when the competition posed by lower-wage countries is increasing.

Another possibility was to extend the duration of CPF retirement payouts beyond 85. But stretching out an individual's savings over a longer period necessarily means reducing the amount of the monthly payouts. It would also require everyone to save for a longer lifespan when not all of them would live beyond 85. Pooling the risks of longevity through an insurance scheme would be a more efficient form of protection.

A third possibility was to encourage individuals to purchase life annuities from commercial insurers, which would then provide some retirement income past the age of 85. While this option was already available, the take-up rate was very low.

---

[2] This comes in the form of monthly payouts from CPF members' accumulated savings.

[3] Before 2007, the drawdown age for CPF members was 62. As part of the 2007 social security reforms, the drawdown age will be increased progressively from 62 to 65. For all members born in the year 1954 or later, their drawdown age will be 65.

In 2007, Prime Minister Lee Hsien Loong mooted the idea of a national annuity scheme in his annual National Day Rally. He explained that because many Singaporeans could expect to live beyond 85, the CPF needed to be reformed to cover this longevity risk, or the risk of outliving one's savings (Lee 2007). An annuity scheme rests on the concept of risk pooling and insurance. The idea was that by pooling a small part of CPF members' retirement savings, the CPF could insure them by providing those who live beyond age 85 with a lifetime stream of income.

In subsequent communications, the government described the possible variations in the design of the proposed annuity scheme. In particular, it highlighted that if payouts were to start at a later age, covering just the tail-end longevity risk, the annuity premium would be lower. This premium could be further reduced if the annuity was designed to have no cash value upon the annuitant's demise, i.e. there would be no refund to the member's beneficiaries. Conscious of the fact that the general features outlined may not meet the diverse needs of Singaporeans, the government embarked on a public consultation exercise to gather views and feedback on the design of the scheme.

The National Longevity Insurance Committee (NLIC) was convened to consider the ideas received from the public, and recommend the final design of the scheme. The Committee took its name from the initial label given to the annuity scheme, the National Longevity Insurance Scheme.

Addressing Public Concerns and Information Gaps

The NLIC's deliberations centred on ensuring an annuity scheme that would be basic, affordable, fair and flexible for CPF members. Designing the scheme required the NLIC to take into account the many concerns of Singaporeans.[4] The next section highlights the

---

[4] More details can be found in the Report by the National Longevity Insurance Committee (2008). In all, more than 600 members of the public contributed to the discussion on the proposed features of the scheme.

key concerns and describes how they were addressed from the perspective of behavioural economics.

Availability Bias

An early and persistent concern was doubt over the published life expectancy figures. Government statistics projected that one in two Singaporeans aged 65 in 2006 would live beyond age 85. But many Singaporeans, when informed that annuity payouts might start at an age later than 65, did not believe that they would live long enough to benefit from the annuity scheme. In views expressed through letters to the national newspapers as well as at the public consultation sessions, some Singaporeans referred to newspaper obituaries as evidence to support their disbelief. This was not surprising since the death notices published in the various dailies were an easily accessible and public source of information. However, obituaries are not representative of the population and are not an accurate guide to future life expectancies. A similar source of biased information would be personal experiences of the recent demise of relatives and friends.

This may well be an example of what behavioural economists call the availability heuristic, where individuals estimate the likelihood of an event by how easily they are able to recall instances or associations (Tversky and Kahneman 1973). It is a heuristic Singaporeans may have relied on when assessing the likelihood of their living beyond age 85. While useful for making snap decisions, the availability heuristic can also lead to systemically biased assessments on issues for which we are ill-equipped to evaluate. Factors such as our personal experiences and how memorable or dramatic the events were can also skew our perceptions of likelihood.

To correct the misperception, NLIC proposed stepping up public education efforts to raise awareness of actual life expectancy and other demographic statistics. Official statistics on life expectancy were highlighted consistently in communications materials used to educate the public on the annuity scheme.

Framing and Loss Aversion

How a policy is framed or presented to the public can also have a significant bearing on how it is received. This was reflected in the concerns that some Singaporeans had over the name of the annuity scheme. The term "longevity insurance" seemed to undermine the public's understanding of what the scheme was intended to achieve. To the man in the street, "insurance" was usually associated with unfortunate events. This was at odds with "longevity", which was something to be celebrated.

The NLIC addressed this concern by reframing the annuity scheme. "Longevity insurance" now became "lifelong income", giving the scheme a positive connotation, while still accurately conveying its basic concept. For easier recall, it was subsequently renamed "CPF Lifelong Income for the Elderly", or CPF LIFE.

LONGEVITY   INSURANCE

Framing. The term "longevity insurance" seemed to undermine the public's understanding of what the scheme was intended to achieve.

A third concern of many individuals was that they would lose out if they were to die early. Such concerns seemed to suggest that individuals were treating the purchase of an annuity like a gamble, in which they were risking their "capital". Their response is an example of what behavioural economists call loss aversion, a phenomenon in which the unhappiness one feels in losing something is greater than the delight felt in acquiring the same thing (Kahneman and Tversky 1979). In the context of the proposed annuity scheme, people tended to place more weight on the risk of losing the premium or "capital", rather than on the potential of gaining additional income beyond the average life expectancy. This aversion to losses could influence individuals' ability to perform an unbiased, rational cost-benefit analysis.

To overcome the problem of CPF members making decisions that focused on potential losses, the NLIC proposed offering plans with premiums that retained some cash value upon the demise of annuitants. Termed "refundable" plans, the beneficiaries of an annuitant could receive a "refund" of the original premium, less the sum of any monthly payouts already received. CPF members could therefore be assured that their "capital" was principal-protected.[5] An additional advantage of refundable plans was that they addressed the desire of many Singaporeans to leave a bequest for their beneficiaries.

Besides the provision of refundable premiums, the NLIC also recommended that individuals be allowed to choose when to commence their annuity payouts. Under their proposal, payouts could start from as early as age 65 to as late as age 90. The option to start receiving payouts as early as age 65 could also help to increase the saliency of potential gains in terms of annuity payouts. If individuals chose to start receiving their annuity payouts from age 65, all their retirement savings would be committed to the annuity plan. On the other hand, if the annuity plan were to start from say age 80, a smaller portion of the individuals' retirement savings would be used to finance the annuity plan. The remaining savings would remain in their CPF accounts and be used to support retirement payouts between age 65 and 80.

---

[5] The trade-off was that such refundable plans would provide a lower stream of income.

Using Defaults

The NLIC eventually recommended a menu of 12 annuity plans to give sufficient flexibility and choice. CPF members could choose from six different ages, at which annuity payouts could start, from 65 to 90 in five-year intervals. Members could also choose between having a refundable or non-refundable premium.

While providing choice was a key goal of the Committee, it also recognised that many people would find the concept of annuities difficult to understand, let alone choose the right plan among the 12 for their own individual circumstances. The Committee therefore designated one of the 12 plans on offer as the default. This plan offered a moderate level of annuity payouts and also satisfied the bequest motive since the premium was refundable. Annuity payouts would start at age 80, an age that many CPF members believed they could conceivably live beyond.

Behavioural economists have written about the importance of defaults, particularly in complex decisions involving risk and uncertainty. Faced with an incomplete or unclear picture, people sometimes make wrong choices, or succumb to inertia and not choose at all. For example, it was conceivable that some CPF members could end up choosing an annuity plan at random. Setting a good default was thus a better policy design than leaving it to chance, while still providing flexibility for those who preferred to exercise active and informed choice to accommodate their own financial situation.

As it turned out, setting a default option was by itself an insufficient measure. The NLIC's proposal of 12 plans still proved confusing for the public, especially since adjacent plans were only marginally different in terms of payout levels and potential bequest amounts. Moreover, members had to grapple with the idea of how the annuity plan would dovetail with their existing CPF savings drawdown plan if they chose a plan that would start annuity payouts after the drawdown age of 65.

Simplifying Choices, Increasing Saliency

A year later, in 2009, the government announced that the number of plans offered would be reduced from twelve to just four, making CPF LIFE simpler to understand while still providing a meaningful set of choices. The four plans were "LIFE Income", "LIFE Plus", "LIFE Balanced" and "LIFE Basic", in descending order of payout levels and ascending order of potential bequest amount. LIFE Income paid the highest income but did not have a bequest feature, while LIFE Basic paid the lowest income but had the highest bequest value. All four plans would start payouts at age 65. As before, one plan was designated as the default, and it was designed to balance the amount of payout with the bequest value of the annuity.

The four plans were a subset of the original twelve proposed by the NLIC. All that had changed was the way CPF LIFE was communicated to the public.

Before the change, members' attention was drawn to the age at which annuity payouts started for each plan. It was the parameter that differentiated one plan from the next. However, members were probably unclear about how the difference in annuity payout start ages translated into the things that mattered most to them: the level of payout they would receive from age 65 onwards and the potential bequest amount.

Public messages were subsequently streamlined to focus on the trade-off between payout level and bequest amount, rather than the different annuity payout start ages (see Exhibit 1 for an example). In addition, the Government emphasised that CPF members would receive an income from CPF Board from age 65, regardless of the plan chosen. These payouts would be funded from the savings that remained in a member's CPF account after a portion of it was deducted for the annuity premium.

The emphasis that payouts would always start from the drawdown age of 65 helped to assure the public that they would be able to enjoy post-retirement income from age 65 onwards and not later as was originally feared. It also reframed and simplified members' decision by highlighting what mattered most to them, while

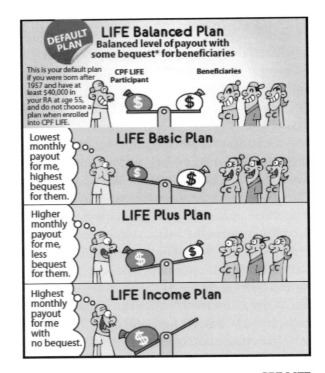

Exhibit 1:   An example of public education messages on CPF LIFE.

de-emphasising what mattered less. CPF members' decisions were now based on a more straightforward comparison between the size of the monthly payout and the bequest amount for one's beneficiaries.

All these refinements contributed to what is termed greater saliency in behavioural economics, or how prominently something stands out. They enabled the government to communicate the concept and the decision parameters of CPF LIFE to the public more easily. Greater saliency of the concept and parameters is also likely to help individuals make better, more informed decisions.

Other Considerations

Other than behavioural considerations in the design of CPF LIFE, it is also important to highlight the costs of operating the scheme. This was a key consideration from the start given that costs would directly impact annuity payout levels. The NLIC and the Government recognised that sufficiently attractive payout levels were a prerequisite to public acceptance of the scheme, even if the concerns over the other features of the scheme were addressed.

Two elements were essential to delivering CPF LIFE at low cost. The first was the inclusive nature of the scheme; the second was that the government would administer it through the CPF Board. Broad-based participation would reduce adverse selection, allow for optimal risk pooling across the large CPF member base, and provide economies of scale in administration. In addition, the non-profit nature of a government administrator and the absence of distribution costs reduce the burden that would otherwise have to be borne by the scheme participants in the form of lower annuity payouts. Yet another advantage of having the CPF Board administer the scheme was that CPF LIFE monies would tap on the CPF interest framework, as the annuity premiums could be invested in special government securities issued only to the CPF Board.

This combination of factors allowed for payouts from the annuity scheme to approximate those from the original withdrawal policy even though the latter would last only about 20 years. In addition, CPF LIFE payouts were more attractive than those offered under similar commercial annuities.

Conclusion

Singapore's experience in implementing CPF LIFE demonstrates the importance of making intelligent use of public feedback to design better policies. Insights from behavioural economics, which augment the principles of conventional economics, helped policymakers understand the public's concerns, refine communication messages, and simplify the choices presented to CPF members. These changes in turn helped Singaporeans to make better decisions to address their old age financial needs.

As a new programme introduced for Singapore's rapidly age-ing population, CPF LIFE is expected to undergo constant refinement and adjustment. Such adaptation has been a hallmark of CPF policies in general, and helps to explain the CPF's central-ity and enduring importance in Singapore's social security architecture. In this adaptive process, behavioural insights will be more important for understanding and meeting the diverse needs of Singaporeans.

References

Akerlof, George and Robert Shiller (2009). *Animal Spirits: How Human Psychology Drives the Economy, and Why it Matters for Global Capitalism.* Princeton University Press.

Department of Statistics, Singapore (2008). "Complete Life Tables 2003–2006 for Singapore Resident Population, February 2008", viewed 1 July 2010, http://www.singstat.gov.sg/pubn/papers/people/ip-s13.pdf.

Kahneman, Daniel and Amos Tversky (1979). "Prospect Theory: An Analysis of Decision under Risk." *Econometrica*, Vol. 47, No. 2, pp. 263–292.

Lee, Hsien Loong (2007). "National Day Rally Speech", viewed 1 July 2010, http://www.pmo.gov.sg/NR/rdonlyres/279CA760-CB50-4438-A878-BA500218C2B1/0/2007NDR_English.doc

National Longevity Insurance Committee (2008). "Report by the National Longevity Insurance Committee", viewed 1 July 2010, http://mycpf.cpf.gov.sg/Members/Gen-Info/CPF_LIFE/NLIC.htm

Tversky, Amos and Daniel Kahneman (1973). "Availability: A Heuristic for Judging Frequency and Probability." *Cognitive Psychology*, Vol. 5, No. 2, pp. 207–232.

CHAPTER 9

BEHAVIOURAL ECONOMICS, POLICY ANALYSIS AND THE DESIGN OF REGULATORY REFORM

Jack KNETSCH

Introduction

In countries where organ donations require the *ex ante* consent of the donor, donations are typically around 20% and much-needed organs are perpetually in short supply. In Canada, for example, even though polling results suggest that 85% of the population were in favour of being an organ donor, only 17% of those people had signed up (Woo and Chai 2011). In other countries including Singapore and parts of Europe, people are presumed to have given consent to donating their organs after death, unless they make an explicit declaration to the contrary. In these countries, the rates of donation are commonly above 80%. Not only is this in line with the public attitude towards organ donations, it also improves society's well-being as the supply of organs is more in keeping with demand and it leads to more lives being saved through timely transplants (Weber 2004).

Most people would not find these observations surprising. They would expect more people to be included in a programme if people had to opt out of it than if they had to opt in. They would also expect people to prefer to have a loss restored than to be provided a gain. This was found when different groups of people — senior Singaporean public servants, international transportation experts and university students in economics classes — were asked to choose between two equally costly transportation projects that would save the same numbers of people the same amount of travel time. The first option was a project that would shorten the distance between two points; the second would replace a failed bridge and eliminate a detour that had increased travel time. Overwhelming majorities in each of the respondent groups favoured the latter project. Importantly, only a few were indifferent between the two options (Chin and Knetsch, forthcoming).

What would surprise most people is that most policy analysts, economists and nearly everyone else involved in designing public policy would find these reactions contrary to their assumptions of people's behaviour. To most economists, a person's decision to donate his organs should depend entirely on whether the person thinks favourably of such an action and not on the default position to which he is assigned. Similarly, whether a project provides a gain or reduces or eliminates a loss should not matter if the amount of gain or loss is identical.

The main reason that the view of most analysts differs from our common sense view is that the former base their understanding of human decisions on standard economic assumptions of rational agents. It is not uncommon for economists to be reminded that, "a failure to satisfy the requirements of economic theory would suggest that the appropriate preferences were not being measured" (Diamond 1996, p. 346); or that "a core set of economic assumptions should be used in calculating benefits and costs" (Arrow *et al.* 1996, p. 222).

The standard tools of traditional economic and policy analyses have provided useful guidance to governments and improved policies and regulations in many countries. Indeed, the consensus among public policy analysts and commentators alike is that our societies would be better served by more widespread use of economic analyses and greater attention to the results.

Much less has been said about the need for better economics and in particular, an economics which is more closely attuned to empirical findings of people's actual behaviours, valuations and choices, as well as how their decisions are influenced by the design of public policies and regulations.

Although seldom commented on until quite recently, the principles of standard economics so widely used in policy analyses are, in a large part, based on quite strong behavioural assumptions: for example, that people have well-formed and stable preferences, that they relentlessly pursue utility maximising behaviour, that they are rational in their pursuits and that money is completely fungible and substitutable over all sources and expenditures.

These assumptions are now increasingly the subject of empirical testing. Recent research by psychologists, economists and other decision scientists has led to a much better appreciation of how people actually choose among alternatives and respond to policy changes. An example is the important finding that people value losses much more than gains of the same size. One experiment showed that people were willing to pay a maximum of $5.60 for a 50% chance to win $20, but they demanded a minimum of $10.87 to give up exactly the same chance (Kachelmeier and Shehata 1992). People have also been shown to have predictable and often strong tendencies to pay undue attention to sunk costs, to anchor on irrelevant reference points, to suffer from self-serving biases, to choose differently when presented with opt-in or opt-out options, to be subject to focusing illusions, to take account of feelings of fairness and to be willing to sacrifice for the benefit of others.

These findings and others contradict standard economic theory and have interesting and important implications for policy decisions. But with the notable exception of behavioural finance, the results from behavioural economics have not yet reached the mainstream of economics textbooks. Neither have they been used in any appreciable way in most countries. This is in spite of behavioural findings being published in every leading professional journal in economics, psychology and related fields; Daniel Kahneman's 2002 Nobel Prize for Economics for his pioneering work in the field; and a vast amount of research pointing to applications over two decades.[1] In short, the application of insights from behavioural research to the design of policies is still the exception rather than the norm among governments.

Behavioural Findings and Policy Design

Much of the research in behavioural economics has focussed on the regularities of people's choices and decisions, particularly those that systematically depart from the predictions of standard economics. Increasing attention is now being given to the implications of these findings and to their use in improving policy and regulatory design (see, for example, Thaler and Sunstein 2008).

An instructive example that led to greatly improved outcomes involves employees' decisions about how much they would contribute to their retirement savings. It is common practice in many countries for new employees to be asked to participate in a company or agency pension plan. Typically, the employees are informed about their expected wages and then asked how much they want deducted from their take-home pay and put into their retirement accounts. In many places, particularly the US and European countries, the saving rates are usually very low and are unlikely to provide a living standard anywhere near that of pre-retirement or what the employee expects.

Based on behavioural findings, Thaler and Benartzi (2004) suggested a straightforward but important variation to this common decision structure. Instead of asking employees how much they wanted to have deducted from their pay — which would be felt as a loss from their reference incomes and therefore resisted — employees

---

[1] It might also be noted that this reluctance to expand the standard view of economics is itself predicted by the behavioural finding that people resist giving up what they have. As the eminent American jurist, Oliver Wendell Holmes put it well over a century ago, "A thing which you have enjoyed and used as your own for a long time, whether property or an opinion, takes root in your being and cannot be torn away without your resenting the act and trying to defend yourself, however you came by it" (1897, p. 477).

were asked to specify how much of their future wage increases they wanted to contribute to their retirement accounts. The decision was thus structured as a foregone gain that employees could agree to more readily.

This simple change was introduced at a medium-sized American firm and the result was dramatic. Contribution to retirement savings went from an average of 3.4% of wages before the change, to 11.6% after and remained at this level. Known as the Save More Tomorrow Programme, it has now been successfully replicated by hundreds of firms with many thousands of employees and has become one of the best-known applications of the findings of behavioural economics.

The approach illustrated here may be applicable in many other cases. In this example, the basic problem of low savings rates was reasonably clear. With the findings of behavioural economics, which warn us of the inhibiting effects of framing something as a loss, it became possible to focus the design of the scheme on circumventing people's loss aversion. Here, this was accomplished by the creative alternative of having the contributions made from future wage increases rather than from current wages. Employees retained the choice of behaving no differently than before, but they were now likely to save more since their contributions would be foregone gains rather than losses from current income. That these contributions would occur in the future rather than at present also made saving much less inhibiting.

A similar approach was used in designing Singapore's national annuity scheme (see Chapter 8). Here too, the objective was clear: to provide income to older Singaporeans who might "outlive" their Central Provident Fund (CPF) retirement savings because of longer life expectancies. The causes of the resistance to the proposed annuity scheme were also identified: the over-weighting of the probability of early death, the fear of losing one's "investment" of contributions, the feared reduction in the size of the bequest to one's beneficiaries and the difficulties of choosing among a complicated myriad of options. As in the case of employees' reluctance to contribute to their retirement savings, once the major behavioural inhibitions to participating in the annuity programme were recognised, the design of the scheme focussed on ways to mitigate their impacts and thus made the scheme more valuable and acceptable to CPF members. The scheme that was eventually adopted simplified choice to only four options and offered choices that guaranteed cash value for beneficiaries in the event of early demise.

Some Further Findings

As more behavioural regularities that depart from standard economics are recognised and confirmed with replicated studies, the range of potential policy applications can be expected to increase. A few examples may help to illustrate this.

Mental Accounting

A common assumption of standard economic theory is that people treat money as completely fungible and that they make their income and expenditure decisions by regarding money across different sources and purposes as completely substitutable. The empirical evidence suggests, however, that people treat monies very differently depending on how it was acquired and what it is to be used for (an excellent review is provided by Thaler (1999)). For instance, most people spend differently on food while on holiday than at home; they treat windfall gains differently from hard-earned cash; they discount capital gains relative to dividends; they increase the tax withheld from their pay cheques to ensure a refund at the end of the year rather than accept a requirement to pay more; and they are willing to spend time to save money on a small purchase but not to save the same sum on a large one. In short, they tend to organise information and make decisions on the basis of their mental accounts.

A suggested reason why corporations declare dividends to shareholders rather than buy up shares to increase their value despite more favourable tax treatment of capital gains in many countries is that people prefer to receive cheques which they then feel free to spend. Retired people are particularly sensitive to this as they like to spend without feeling that they are dipping into their capital (Thaler 1999).

Another example of mental accounting is the way prepayment and other payment devices often have the effect of "decoupling" payment from consumption. Resorts, for example, often charge fixed prices that include multiple items, the purchase of which would be resisted if they had to be paid for separately. People also prefer to pay a flat fee rather than have the "meter running", not only for taxi rides but also for many other services. Perhaps the most well known decoupling device is the credit card which, in addition to convenience, offers consumers a simple way to separate purchase from payment. The result is that consumers feel less restrained than if immediate cash outlay was required for each purchase.

A policy implication of the decoupling phenomenon arises with the use of automatic toll collection or congestion charging devices. In most instances, the toll or congestion charges are either automatically deducted from a card in the vehicle or they are consolidated in monthly bills sent to vehicle owners. Whatever the convenience and engineering cleverness of these devices, one of the results is to decouple the use of roads at socially disadvantageous times from the payment for it. This almost certainly compromises the effectiveness of tolls and congestion charges in shifting demand and encouraging more efficient use of roads, maybe seriously so. Efforts such as the prominent display of the real-time congestion charges on hard-to-ignore display boards in Singapore can help to mitigate these decoupling impacts (see Chapter 3).

The disincentive effects of tolls may also be strengthened by paying more attention to other behavioural factors. For example, it may be helpful to frame the toll more explicitly as the price to cover the external costs that each vehicle imposes on others by way of congestion-induced delay, pollution, increased risk of accidents and the like. The importance of the usually modest sums paid in tolls could also be increased by framing these expenditures more narrowly. Instead of presenting the charges as a very small percentage of a person's total income — and therefore easily ignored — transport planners could frame the toll or congestion charges as a proportion of people's transport-related expenditures, thus making them appear larger, more salient and more effective as a deterrent.

Sunk Cost Effect

Another case of mental accounting is the fixed or sunk cost effect. Standard economics assumes that people ought to and actually do, ignore sunk costs. Economics teaches that once an expense is made, it is sunk and decisions should be based only on marginal gains and losses from that point on. However, the evidence again suggests that most people often do otherwise. They are more likely to endure a blizzard to go to a sporting event if they have already purchased a ticket than if they have not (Thaler 1999). And the more they have paid for a season ticket to performances of a theatre group, the more likely people are to go to every event (Arkes and Blumer 1985).[2]

The propensity to try to "recover" our sunk costs can also have a marked impact on the use of vehicles. Many countries manage car population and use with a mix of purchase and operating taxes and charges. However, very high fixed charges can have quite the opposite effect from the intended one of curtailing car use — people who have paid high purchase taxes often feel they have to drive more to justify this expenditure and "spread the cost out over more trips". This then worsens rather than ameliorates traffic congestion and pollution. In contrast, a high tax on the marginal use of a vehicle would be more effective in reducing car usage, as people are then more transparently faced with the marginal cost of each trip.

The opposite framing and impacts of these two types of taxes suggest that if the aim is to limit vehicle use (at certain times and at particular places), then fixed cost taxes should be reduced or eliminated and variable taxes (such as those on fuel, or better, on the actual distance travelled at particular times and places) should be greatly increased.

Singapore, for example, used to impose very high fixed cost taxes on vehicle purchase and registration —— with the conse-quence that it has one of the highest rates of distance travelled per car in the world despite the country's small size. There was, how-ever, growing recognition of the unintended incentives created by these policies and in recent years, the government has lowered fixed cost taxes and raised variable taxes (see Chapter 3). But the changes have been relatively modest and the world-leading driv-ing rates seem to be continuing.

---

[2] Attention to sunk costs can also have more tragic consequences, as in cases when continuations of armed conflicts are supported with the persuasive appeal that cessation of hostilities would mean that people killed earlier "would have died in vain".

The Power of Free

Standard economics treats zero as just another price, no different from any other. People, however, frequently treat "free" quite differently from other prices.

The well-known choice-of-chocolate experiment is an instructive demonstration of the power of free. When both a premium Lindt truffle (15 cents) and a more ordinary Hershey's Kiss (1 cent) were offered to a group of participants, only a quarter of the participants (27%) purchased the Hershey. But when the prices of both were reduced by 1 cent, making the Hershey's Kiss free, two-thirds (67%) then went for it (Shampanier *et al.* 2007).

A similar dramatic change was observed when a positive charge was imposed on a formerly free service. A Canadian municipal library began charging for online reservations of books to be picked up later when notified of their availability. The introduction of a nominal 50-cent service fee resulted in the average monthly number of requests dropping from 7,079 per month for the ten months prior to implementation of the charge, to 2,703 per month for the five months after — a 62% decrease (personal communication with North Vancouver library staff).

While some commercial marketing schemes have incorporated an element of a "free something" in their offers, in the realm of public policy there has been a reluctance to harness the power of free to promote socially desirable choices. For example, offering free registration for less polluting cars might encourage more buyers to choose them. Or, as has been done in Melbourne (Currie 2010), offering free use of public transit systems during off-peak times might effectively reduce the costly narrow peaks in usage and spread them over a longer time period. The loss of fare revenues may be (partially) offset by the reduced need for rolling stock, while generating non-financial benefits in the form of more comfortable commutes for all. Here, as in many cases, the aim is not to shift the bulk of riders, only enough to smooth the use for all and to provide a more efficient service.

Disparity between Gains and Losses

The evidence that people frequently value losses much more than gains is perhaps the most extensive of all behavioural findings and certainly among the most important. This phenomenon is very much at odds with the predictions of standard economics, but a wide array of replicated survey studies, carefully controlled experiments involving real money exchanges and recordings of people's daily decisions reported over the past three decades have provided overwhelming evidence of systematic, large and pervasive differences (see, for example, Kahneman *et al.* 1990; Rabin 1998; and Horowitz and McConnell 2002).

A well known example of the valuation disparity is the finding that only 10% of people given a decorated coffee mug would exchange it for a large chocolate bar and only 11% given the chocolate bar would exchange it for a mug (Knetsch 1989). People demonstrated that whatever item they had in their possession became more valuable than the alternative when faced with the possibility of losing it in a costless trade. Similar evidence is provided by Putler's (1992) finding that shoppers were much more sensitive to an increase in the price of eggs (price elasticity of –1.10) which imposes a loss than they were to a reduction in price (elasticity of only –0.45) which provides a gain. In short, people's consumption is reduced a lot more by a price rise than it is increased by a price fall.

The often wide disparity between people's valuations of gains and of losses[3] obviously has major implications for policy design. For instance, loss aversion helps to explain the difference in outcomes when various options are designated as the default. As in the chocolate and mug experiment noted above, people are reluctant to give up something they own for an alternative as the loss looms larger than the potential gain.

---

[3] Horowitz and McConnell (2002) found in their review of 45 studies that the median valuation of losses was 2.6 times more than the gains (while the mean ratio was approximately 7 times).

WHEN IT'S
NOT MINE,
VALUE = $

WHEN IT'S
MINE,
VALUE = $$

This phenomenon was observed in a study of vehicle owners in two US states — Pennsylvania and New Jersey — who were offered the choice of two insurance options. One option was considerably less expensive but restricted recovery in the event of an accident; the other was more expensive but had fewer restrictions. Both options were nearly identical in the two states, but in Pennsylvania the more expensive policy was the default, while in New Jersey the cheaper policy was the default. Even though changing out of the default would incur no transaction costs, only 20% of the vehicle owners in New Jersey and 25% in Pennsylvania switched out of their respective defaults. Thus 20% in New Jersey and 75% in Pennsylvania ended up with the more expensive and less restrictive policy. Since there is no reason to expect vehicle owners in the two states to have widely differing insurance preferences, the 55 percentage point difference seems clearly the result of the default rule (Johnson *et al.* 1993).

The Choice of Measure to Value Changes

Most policymakers accept that the impact on economic welfare should be a major consideration when assessing policy options. Standard economics says that when measuring the increase in economic welfare resulting from an improvement, the policy analyst should try to determine the maximum sum that the beneficiaries are willing to pay (WTP) for the improvement. Similarly, to measure the reduction in welfare resulting from a loss, the policy analyst should estimate the minimum amount that the victims would require as compensation to accept the loss, i.e. the person's willingness to accept (WTA). However, in policy and regulatory design, or when choosing between different projects, the common practice in government is to determine the welfare effects of all changes by the WTP measure, regardless of whether the change is a gain or a loss. So even where individuals suffer a loss, the reduction in welfare is often measured by their WTP to avoid, or to reduce, the loss.

This deviation from agreed principle has been justified by the assumption of standard economics that the two measures will result in equivalent valuations, except for a small difference due to the income effect. This assumption has led to the choice of measure being largely a matter of convenience or ease of measurement, with little attention given to the *appropriateness* of the choice. For example, in its guidelines for economic analyses, the US Environmental Protection Agency observes that "in practice, the WTP is generally used to value benefits because it is often easier to measure and estimate" (US EPA 2000).[4] A consequence is the continuing practice of valuing all changes with the WTP measure, e.g. "the value of a statistical life...is the willingness to pay for a reduction in mortality risk" (Krupnick 2007, p. 261).

The now widely observed disparity between people's valuations of gains and losses calls into question the claim of equivalence between the WTA and WTP measures. It also raises important questions about what criteria we should use to determine the appropriate measure. This can be illustrated by a simple thought experiment involving the blocking of a roadway by an

---

[4] This is particularly the case when stated preference or contingent valuation methods are used to estimate values — as they have been in many environmental changes and increasingly in other areas such as transportation and health. Getting respondents to give meaningful answers to questions asking for how much compensation they would demand to accept a loss is perceived as difficult. This has resulted in the use of WTP estimates in essentially all such studies regardless of the gain or loss nature of the change.

overturned lorry. The stopping of traffic is clearly a loss imposed on motorists and is therefore most accurately assessed with the WTA measure — the minimum sum motorists would want to be compensated to accept the blockage. Most motorists would view the re-opening of the road to traffic as eliminating the harm rather than as a gain. The restoration of normal traffic flow would therefore be more accurately assessed with their WTA to forego it and not with their willingness to pay for it (Knetsch *et al.* forthcoming).

Why is the standard practice of using WTP to determine the value of the mitigation measure inappropriate? Because it implies that the overturned lorry and being stranded behind a barrier of spilled freight is the "normal" state and the payment is to improve what is normal. This point of view, while possible, is improbable. Motorists are far more likely to see the clearing of the road as a return to their reference of free-flowing traffic.

Given the pervasiveness of large disparities between WTA and WTP valuations of a change, the improper choice of measure could result in seriously biased guidance. In turn, this can lead to the unintended encouragement of activities with negative social impacts such as pollution and risks to health and safety, improper restitution for injuries, unduly lax deterrence disincentives and too little mitigation of harms.

Policy and the Creation of Feelings of Entitlement

Another often unanticipated result of implementing a policy is the resulting feelings of entitlement on the part of beneficiaries and the consequent accumulation of interests in maintaining the flow of benefits. This entitlement problem may arise when the benefits of a public policy or project are capitalised in the value of privately owned fixed assets — very often land — with little further benefit accruing to others (Tullock 1975). For example, when public agencies build irrigation works or distribute free or under-priced irrigation water to privately owned agricultural lands, the beneficiaries are usually the farmers who are able to sell greatly increased quantities of produce. However, because the irrigation water is tied to specific parcels of land, the value of the land parcels also increases due to the increased net value of current and future production. This often happens immediately after such projects are announced. Buyers are willing to pay more because the land is now capable of producing more and the seller demands higher prices to give up the increased stream of profits made possible by the irrigation water.

Such capitalisation also occurs when authorities award special privileges to individuals or groups, such as taxicab licences that confer the right to transport people for a price, fishing quotas, agricultural crop price guarantees, or pollution permits. The common characteristics of such awards include:

- the privilege allows the generation of higher returns (bigger crop yields, catching more fish, generating more pollution, etc.);
- the increase in the value of output becomes capitalised in the value of the asset that conveys the privilege (the taxicab licence, the land receiving the irrigation water, the licence permitting the activity, the boat to which a fishing quota is attached, etc.);
- the owners of the asset receiving the privilege will be the primary and usually the sole beneficiary of the scheme as any subsequent owner will need to pay a price that reflects the full (discounted) value of all future returns of the increased productivity; and
- both the original recipients of the privilege and the current owners will strongly resist cessation of the programme as this would erode the value of the asset due to the capitalisation of anticipated future returns.

The finding that people often value losses more than commensurate gains may provide insights into how policies may create feelings of entitlement. For example, if the policy fosters the expectation that the privilege is a recurring or continuing one, it is likely to encourage people to view the reference state as one in which the privilege is maintained. Subsequently, any attempt to alter this reference state will be viewed as a much more aversive loss and hence strongly resisted. At the same time, behavioural insights also suggest how policies can be designed in ways that prevent, or at least discourage, the perception of the privilege as a continuing benefit that justifies a shift of the reference state.

The design of discretionary fiscal transfers in Singapore reflects an awareness of these considerations (see Chapter 6). Many of these transfers sought to provide income supplements to people while avoiding the negative consequences arising from the expectation of a permanent entitlement. While the government's surplus-sharing programmes were designed partly to meet redistributive objectives, it also sought to discourage any expectation that these transfers would become the norm. These programmes often take the form of in-kind contributions to savings, health, housing, or training/education schemes, rather than outright cash payments; they are nearly always framed as "one-off" special distributions to the point of being classified in the Budget as "special transfers". The success of the various programmes may vary, but the intent of discouraging feelings of entitlement and the consequent shifts in people's reference states has been quite clear.

The Appeal of Dedicated Funds (Earmarking)

It has long been a firm principle of public finance that monies collected for the use of public facilities should be credited to general public revenue accounts that can be used for whatever purposes deemed to be socially most desired. The alternative of earmarking or devoting revenues collected from a service to specific uses related to that service is generally discouraged by economists. The rationale for this is that the necessarily narrower focus is likely to result in the agency using the money for a purpose that is less valuable than if it could be allocated to an alternative public use. Money collected for the use of a park, for example, might be better used in providing healthcare than in expanding parks. And funds from road tolls might be better used to hire more food inspectors than to build more roads.

For the same reason, conventional economics suggests that all else being equal, compensation for harms will normally be more efficient than mitigation actions to reduce or eliminate the harms. The reasoning is analogous in that the mitigation action deals only with whatever has been injured whereas compensation payments allow recipients to use the funds for whatever good or service is most valuable to them — which may well be something unrelated to the thing that was originally harmed.

Yet people's reactions in many cases have been found to be seriously at variance with this principle. People appear to prefer that the money they pay for a service be returned in some form related to that service. Such earmarked funds are also less likely to be seen as a government "money grab". For example, it has been found that users of public parks and campgrounds are much more accepting of an increase in entrance or user fees, if the money collected is used to improve the facilities they were using than if it was put into general government revenues. In Singapore, it is also quite common for members of the public to ask for vehicle-related taxes and the revenue from congestion charging to be "put back" into improving roads or the public transport system.

Loss aversion offers a partial explanation for people's preference for mitigation remedies over compensation. People tend to view compensation less favourably because while it offers them a gain (which is discounted for being such), it leaves them with the injury — a loss on which people place a greater value. The mitigation measure is more likely to be viewed as reducing the loss and therefore valued more.

The strength of this distinction has been borne out in surveys and experimental studies, as well as in the observations of the reactions of injured parties. For example, when given a choice between two remedies for a minor environmental harm, (a) an order for the responsible party to undertake what would be a partially effective mitigation action, or (b) an order for the party to compensate the community with a like sum for "whatever use is decided on by local residents in a referendum", 70% of respondents favoured spending large sums of money on the first option which by definition would not do much good, rather than use the expenditure to get something they really wanted (Knetsch 1990, p. 233).

Fairness and Other-Regarding Behaviour

Standard economics also suggests that people seek to maximise their personal welfare with little regard for others outside of their immediate household. Here too, the empirical evidence suggests that regard for others and feelings of what is and is not fair influence the actions and choices of most people. While standard analysis has taken account of issues of vertical equity — the treatment of and consequences for, the poor relative to rich — there has been much less explicit regard for issues of horizontal equity, or the like treatment of people in similar circumstances to oneself. The latter has been the subject of some empirical research and the findings suggest that some simple rules dictate much of what people regard as fair dealings (Kahneman *et al.* 1986).

One rule seems to be that it is generally unfair for one party to gain at the direct expense of another. In a random household survey of Canadians and confirmed by later studies in other countries, respondents were asked to judge the fairness of different approaches taken by a department store to sell its one remaining toy doll. A large majority of respondents judged holding an auction to secure the highest profit to be unfair, as the store would benefit at the expense of the customer. However, when respondents were told that the added profit would go to a charity, the auction was then judged to be fair because the store was not seen as benefiting at the expense of its customers.

It also appears to be unfair for one party to exploit circumstances to increase profits. For instance, large majorities of respondents judged it to be very unfair for a landlord to impose a higher increase in rent if he knew that the tenant had taken a job nearby and would therefore be unlikely to move. But at the same time, most people felt it was fair for landlords (and others) to pass on cost increases. They also felt it was fair for employers to share losses by cutting the wages of their employees, but thought it was very unfair if the firm was still profitable.

While most of the findings on fairness judgments have come from North America and Europe, there are also now findings from Asia and other areas. The striking feature of these disparate studies is the similarity in responses and judgments, suggesting that fairness judgements may well cut across different cultures.

While fairness motivations and people's regard for others are not usually considered explicitly in policy decisions, there is now considerable evidence that they influence a wide range of people's behaviours. For instance, sticky wages are a widely observed phenomenon all over the world. Not only do employees resist wage cuts, there is also wide agreement in society that it is unfair to impose such losses on workers (unless the employer can show that losses are being incurred). The same resistance does not appear to be prompted by cuts to annual bonuses (because these are viewed as foregone gains). This suggests that wage flexibility can be increased by greater use of bonuses as part of workers' pay packets. Countries such as Singapore, where bonuses are a relatively large part of workers' compensation, thus enjoy a macroeconomic advantage over others that have less flexible wage systems.

There is also surprisingly consistent regard for fairness in other domains. For instance, prices generally reflect changes in costs more closely than shifts in demand, as it is almost unquestionably fair to pass on the higher costs along with a fair profit. On the other hand, increasing prices to take advantage of an increase in demand is often regarded as unfair "price gouging". Fairness considerations might therefore act as a constraint that prevents some markets — such as those for resorts in peak holiday periods — from clearing when there are significant increases in demand.

Conclusion

Although there remains much to be done to apply behavioural findings to the design and implementation of public policies, it is already clear that the quality of debate and decision making in policy design can be significantly enhanced by more attention to these findings. Governments would be better placed to set priorities that are in keeping with the preferences of their citizens. They would also be able to formulate policies that are more likely to achieve their intended outcomes and attain greater public acceptance. Behavioural economics is not a substitute for standard economic analyses, but it appears on present evidence to be a most useful supplement to it — a way of practising better economics and better policy analysis.

References

Arkes, Hal and Catherine Blumer (1985). "The Psychology of Sunk Cost." *Organizational Behavior and Human Decision Processes*, Vol. 35, No. 1, pp. 124–140.

Arrow, Kenneth, Maurine Cropper, George Eads, Robert Hahn, Lester Lave, Roger Noll, Paul Porney, Milton Russell, Richard Schmalensee, V. Kerry Smith and Robert Stavins (1996). "Is there a Role for Benefit-Cost Analysis in Environmental, Health and Safety Regulation?" *Science*, Vol. 272, No. 5259, pp. 221–222.

Chin, Anthony and Jack Knetsch (forthcoming). "The Choice of Measure Matters: Are Many Transport Project Valuations Seriously Biased?"

Currie, Graham (2010). "Quick and Effective Solution to Rail Overcrowding: Free 'Early Bird' Ticket Experience in Melbourne, Australia." *Transportation Research Record*, No. 2146, pp. 35–42.

Diamond, Peter (1996). "Testing the Internal Consistency of Contingent Valuation Surveys." *Journal of Environmental Economics and Management*, Vol. 30, No. 3, pp. 337–347.

Holmes, Oliver (1897). "The Path of the Law." *The Harvard Law Review*, Vol. 10, pp. 457–478.

Horowitz, John and Kenneth McConnell (2002). "A Review of WTA/WTP Studies." *Journal of Environmental Economics and Management*, Vol. 44, No. 3, pp. 426–447.

Johnson, Eric, John Hershey, Jacqueline Meszaros and Howard Kunreuther (1993). "Framing Probability Distortions, and Insurance Decisions." *Journal of Risk and Uncertainty*, Vol. 7, No. 1, pp. 35–51.

Kachelmeier, Steven and Mohd. Shehata (1992). "Examining Risk Preferences Under High Monetary Incentives: Experimental Evidence from the People's Republic of China." *American Economic Review*, Vol. 82, No. 5, pp. 1120–1141.

Kahneman, Daniel, Jack Knetsch and Richard Thaler (1986). "Fairness as a Constraint on Profit Seeking: Entitlements in the Market." *American Economic Review*, Vol. 76, No. 4, pp. 728–741.

Kahneman, Daniel, Jack Knetsch and Richard Thaler (1990). "Experimental Tests of the Endowment Effect and the Coase Theorem." *Journal of Political Economy*, Vol. 98, No. 6, pp. 1325–1348.

Knetsch, Jack (1989). "The Endowment Effect and Evidence of Nonreversibile Indifference Curves." *The American Economic Review*, Vol. 79, No. 5, pp. 1277–1284.

Knetsch, Jack (1990). "Environmental Policy Implications of Disparities Between Willingness to Pay and Compensation Demanded Measures of Values." *Journal of Environmental Economics and Management*, Vol. 18, No. 3, pp. 227–237.

Knetsch, Jack, Yohanes Eko Riyanto and Zong Jichuan (forthcoming). "The Choice of Measures to Value Increases and Decreases in the Domain of Gains and in the Domain of Losses."

Krupnick, Alan (2007). "Mortality-Risk Valuation and Age: Stated Preference Evidence." *Review of Environmental Economics and Policy*, Vol. 1, No. 2, pp. 261–282.

Putler, Daniel (1992). "Incorporating Reference Price Effects Into a Theory of Consumer Choice." *Marketing Science*, Vol. 11, No. 3, pp. 287–309.

Rabin, Matthew (1998). "Psychology and Economics." *Journal of Economic Literature*, Vol. 36, No. 1, pp. 11–46.

Shampanier, Kristina, Nina Mazar and Dan Ariely (2007). "Zero as a Special Price: The True Value of Free Products." *Marketing Science*, Vol. 26, pp. 742–757.

Thaler, Richard (1999). "Mental Accounting Matters." *Journal of Behavioral Decision Making*, Vol. 12, No. 3, pp.183–206.

Thaler, Richard and Shlomo Benartzi (2004). "Save More Tomorrow: Using Behavioral Economics to Increase Employee Saving." *Journal of Political Economy*, Vol. 112, No. 1, S164–S182.

Thaler, Richard and Cass Sunstein (2008). *Nudge: Improving Decisions About Health, Wealth and Happiness*. Yale University Press.

Tullock, Gordon (1975). "The Transitional Gains Trap." *The Bell Journal of Economics*, Vol. 6, No. 2, pp. 671–678.

US Environmental Protection Agency (2000). *Guidelines for Preparing Economic Analyses*. Washington D.C.

Weber, Elke (2004). "Who's Afraid of a Poor Old Age? Risk Perception in Risk Management Decisions," in Olivia Mitchell and Stephen Utkus, eds., *Pension Design and Structure: New Lessons from Behavioral Finance*. Oxford University Press.

Woo, Andrea and Carmen Chai (2011). "Shortage of Donor Kidneys Taxes Health Care." *Vancouver Sun*, 21 January, p. B3.

INDEX